THE VALUE
MATRIX 2.0

THE VALUE MATRIX 2.0

The binary nature of economic and social values

Guido George Lombardi

CONTENTS

"To change, we first have to change our perceptions."
From *The Seven Habits of Highly Effective People*
by Stephen Covey

INTRODUCTION

Today, at the dawn of the twenty-first century, we set eyes on a world in rapid change. In order to adjust and lead these changes, we need to clearly understand what we want and what we value. We must go to the roots of our needs and desires, from the most basic ones, like food and shelter, to higher and nobler aspirations, like justice and freedom.

Food: that ever-present desire. Tasty, delicious, invigorating food, the stuff we cannot live without . . . literally. Have you ever tried a 16-course dinner at a fine French restaurant 20 miles outside of Paris? What about six hours of endless food, wines and aromas (complete with live popular music and songs) at an Italian wedding feast in the hills of Tuscany? And what about those big Thanksgiving meals?

I hope you like variety, because this book is a little like that, written with a variety of styles and expressions; some are plain, like doughnuts and French fries; others are more technical, for those who like precise jargon, classical music, Russian caviar, or the works of Renoir.

And, like those memorable meals, you only get one every so often. But too many flavors may spoil the soup. This mix of flavors and ideas—some old but often winning, some new and exotic, a few outside of any paradigm—has been written with defects in arrangement and some repetition. For those and for any other shortcomings, I apologize to the reader.

We all have desires. We all have needs, sometimes different ones. We all value different things and people. We value health, wealth (and all the things that money can buy), success, passion (love, sex, relationships, and all that they involve), security (financial as well as personal security), beauty, friendship, honesty, honor, justice, freedom, and a host of other things. But how do these values come about?

In this book, I am taking you on a wild journey of thought and reflection, looking for a code that can unlock the real meaning of value.

You have heard of value-added products and services, but what is the source of these and of other types of value? And, since value permeates most of our lives (not only in an economic sense), what are the values that are truly lasting, and those that are only transient?

These questions I have tried to answer with a few findings, summarized in what I call *the new value matrix*, based on a binary approach: *a binary value system.*

Very often, values determine behavior and, in developing this new value matrix, I have found some interesting and useful insights into the way men and women behave.

This new theory is hard to summarize in a few sentences. It contains a variety of approaches and viewpoints, some of which you may agree with, and some, you may not. But that is fine, because in this smorgasbord of ideas I am quite certain that you will find some tasty piece of wisdom, something to enjoy, some insight, something useful for you personally (for your family, or your job), something to quench a little of your mind's thirst, some resonance that will linger on long after you close this book.

And, like your Sunday brunch, there may be lots of good information in this book, but not everyone may want to read it all. So, I divided the good stuff, the meat and potatoes, from the more boring and technical notes, which you will find in the form of endnotes at the end of each chapter.

What do you want? What do you need? I believe that we all need (among other things) some refreshing new idea. We need some new parameter that can help us see more clearly where we stand and where we can go, both in our personal lives and in our communities. We need to clear the table of some old, foolish assumptions and superstitions in order to make room for clearer, nourishing views of the brand new world in which we live.

On the evening news, we often witness war, conflicts, and struggles, but at the heart of wars and fights are the clashing values of opposing groups.

The title speaks for itself. I have tried to formulate a comprehensive (alas, superficial) exposition on "value," what real value is, how human beings perceive themselves and the world, and how men and women relate (not always harmoniously) to each other and to things based on their value-system (their all-important value matrix), and why it is important, in order to have successful and profitable relations, to share some basic values and common rules of behavior.

Over the past two decades, most businesses (and other organizations) have understood the importance of continuous learning as a competitive strategy. But, up to now, learning had been locked in an antiquated and now crumbling structure. Real knowledge, and indeed wisdom, is becoming the right of the learner, and not, as it has been in the past, the privilege of the teacher. With the advent of the Internet, we have witnessed an incredible growth in the "learning" and technological expertise of key industries, from consumer products to heavy industries and from schools to homes.

Enormous amounts of information have become available to multitudes of people all over the planet. Now we need to learn how to sort the data and choose among endless scenarios. By proposing a new way of understanding values, by proposing a new worldview (both in economic and social terms), I hope to be a facilitator—one who provides new choices and empowering options, one voice pointing to positive new possibilities for our destinies.

The *Information Age* is transforming itself into the *Knowledge Age*, and now we must learn to choose the type of knowledge that is best for our purposes, the best kind of long-term, workable knowledge: wisdom.

Look out for value-added information and for valuable knowledge. Look out for the coming *Age of Wisdom.*

CHAPTER I

FROM BRASILIA TO NEW YORK

What do we value?

The sun was scorching. The air was spicy. Even the mud was hot. Marcon was digging for gold in the new pit. He was covered with mud, hungry, tired, one hundred miles from Brasilia and from his wife and kids. He was shoveling the musty dirt with dozens of other desperate men, hoping to find that big nugget that would change his life. In the distance, under a shanty roof, the armed guards were listening to samba on the radio.

A few thousand miles away, in New York City, Frank arrived late at his trading desk, on the 27th floor of the World Financial Center, next to where the Twin Towers once stood. He almost spilled the coffee he got from Starbuck's. "Turn on the TV!" he screamed at Jack. "It's already seven o'clock. I need to see CNBC in the morning." It was going to be another hot day in the Big Apple. Hopefully, he'd get some action and sell some stocks.

The other brokers were breathing down his neck. He needed some big bonus to make the down payment for the new house.

From the vibrant green forests of Brazil, where hordes of dreamers dig deep for gold in the hot Amazon's forest, to the concrete and steel jungles of Wall Street, where multitudes of people from every nationality crowd into the steamy streets to pursue their dream, every human being struggles with the new global economy. We live in the best of times and in a time with the greatest of opportunities, a time when humanity has reached the point of no return in the establishment of one global village.

The world is wired together, looking more and more like one giant information network, one global "nervous system," as Bill Gates describes it in his book, *Business @ the Speed of Thought*. The globe is one interconnected economic system, where everyone, to one degree or another, is a consumer, a maker and a partaker in the making of the world economy. And everyone (some more, some less) searches for "economic value." We all try to make a little (or a lot) more money in order to get the things we want and improve the quality of our lives.

For these reasons, it is most important, at this time, to begin the search for a more humane and globally acceptable economic system, one that will help unify and harmonize existing national economies into a truly global and peaceful village.

Some values change, other values endure the test of time. It is essential to understand one's own values and the values of one's opposing parties (be it for the purpose of winning them over or for defeating them).

In order to find unity and cooperation, we need to find common values; to find economic success, we need to understand the root of economic value.

Some economists, among whom I hope we can count Mr. Allan Greenspan, Chairman of the Federal Reserve Board, believe that the foundations of economic well being in the 21st century must rest on the basic humanitarian principles and moral rectitude of future economic policies and not on the financial re-shuffling of outdated ideas centered on greed.

I believe that *the key, as always, lies in our own hands, and that key is connected to what we value and what we believe: our value system, our value matrix.*

So this is the meaning of this book. In it, I recorded my findings on my search for value, not just economic value, not just the value of things, rather, I decided to study the source of value—how and why we value things. Why do we value certain kinds of people? Why do we hold on so tight to some beliefs and traditions (we obviously "value" them highly) while we quickly disregard others? What is it that makes something more valuable than something else?

Why do we value a 10-carat diamond ring? Or a great dinner at Sirio Maccioni's *Le Cirque Restaurant* on 51st street in Manhattan? Why do we value the smiling face of Maria Bartiromo on CNBC, telling us the early morning "expectations" of the market (and that our stocks have gone up through the roof)? And what about the value of our health? What about the value of the fresh morning air, a walk in the park, the loving drawing of our five-year-old child, the sweet smell of flowers, the unexpected phone call of a loved one, or the deep rhythms of familiar music and songs?

Music and songs are common to every culture. We value them, and we value the meanings we give them.

Sometimes, when listening to music, parts of your life seem to flash in front of your eyes. That's because music and songs capture meaningful moments, feelings and emotions. Music captures states of mind and sentiments connected to meaningful and valuable events and people. That's why music has value.

But how do we value all other things? Where does economic value come from?

In 1929, the market crash heralded the Great Depression. In 1987, there was the now infamous "Black Monday." In 1999, there was Allan Greenspan's famous reference to the "irrational exuberance" of the stock market, which started the wide swings of the Dow and the NASDAQ. Tomorrow . . . who knows?

Bottom line: Nobody can tell us what the future of the economy will be for certain.

Even the work of two Nobel Prize winners, Professors James Heckman and Daniel McFadden, is not sufficient to understand the real forces behind economic development and technological innovation. According to the Royal Swedish Academy of the Sciences, the two Nobel laureates were rewarded for "developing theory and methods that are widely used in the statistical analysis of individuals and households."

Other economists may investigate Dr. Heckman's study on the motivation of individuals choosing to respond to opinion polls and other statistical studies and Dr. McFadden's work on the economic reasons for individual choices. Suffice it to say here that one of the principal *assumptions,* and, in my humble opinion, one very *unproven assumption*, of these and other macroeconomic theories is that "people will always act so as to maximize their self-interest."

As we will see in later chapters, human needs, desires, wants and aspirations are *not* driven exclusively by cold and selfish economic considerations, quite the contrary, economic motivation is not sufficient in itself to explain a value theory.

Another economic assumption that must be challenged is that markets operate efficiently. This work has earned three other Americans, Joseph Stiglits, Michael Spence, and George Akerlof, the latest Nobel for economics. But, if you read the boring details, you'll find nothing new there. You'll find critiques of old theories but no answers or solutions.

Innovation, change, and revolution seem to be the passwords of this age. The post-modern age, a little less than a century old, from the end of World War One in 1918 to the first decade of the third millennium, has certainly witnessed the greatest and fastest changes in human society.

Every aspect of our global culture has faced challenges, every underlying value has been put to the test (particularly after 9/11/ 2001). And that is fine, because, at a certain point of their history, all people and all nations feel the need to rediscover their own soul, their proper identity. This leads them to renew some of their traditional values and replace others with new ideals, new values and new rules.

All of us, both as individuals and as communities, need ideals, values and a positive vision of the future that can energize and propel us toward better and higher lives.

Some of my early studies have been in philosophy, with less than 10 years of informal training in strategic and organizational planning and a little more than two decades of practical experience in the business arena. For these reasons, this book, whose lofty goal is a revolutionary, new theory of value, is limited to what I consider the root of the economic science: its philosophical foundations and its teleological implications and not its hard mathematical representations. This doesn't mean that there are no boring parts, but I have tried to keep the technical jargon down to a minimum. The bottom line is the search for innovative ideas and a new vision for a responsible global economy in the 21st century: the new value matrix.

REAL CHANGE

What do we need?

Have you ever watched Oprah Winfrey? The first time I noticed her and her show, I was intrigued by the way she talked to people with a weight problem. Listening carefully, you could detect the very clever ways in which she led people into accepting their problem. Then, she found ways to motivate them to make a change. There is no doubt that one of the keys to her success has been her ability to convey some of the tools that people need to change their lives.

Real changes start with a change in our values and norms, our worldviews, and our beliefs. The importance of values, both tangible and intangible, has been clearly identified not only in economics, but also in every aspect of society and in every culture. Different cultural value systems and contrasting traditions are facing each other every moment in newspapers and magazines, and on television and Internet screens the world over.

As the world becomes more like a single global village, we will continue to witness an unequivocal convergence and flattening of values. The automatic result of this continuous exposure to different cultures is the alignment and leveling off of global values and the development of a "common denominator," a system of globally acceptable values (please note that I do not advocate accepted values, but merely acceptable, tolerable ones).

The answer to the clash between opposing values is a new paradigm, a new way in which to perceive and value ourselves, other people, our society, and all things that surround us. Even motivational trainers and coaches, from Tony Robbins to football legend Vince Lombardi (no, we are not related), teach that the first step towards success is a positive evaluation of yourself ("value and believe in yourself").

We need to replace old assumptions, such as man's selfish nature and his so-called "rational" behavior, with a greater sense of community values and a new rational behavior inclusive of the community and the environment.

Having challenged these and other basic assumptions of the capitalist and Marxist paradigms, we can see that human beings are endowed, by their very nature, not only with certain inalienable rights, but also with a certain common character (both a selfish as well as more noble nature), that makes all human beings similar to one another, members of one single species, one human family.

THE ECONOMIC VALUE
OF CONSERVATION

What else do we need?

It was five o'clock in the afternoon, and we were having tea and cookies on a big terrace, a few yards away from the ocean in

Caneel Bay, just above St. John's northern beach, in the Virgin Islands. The sun was low, and the ocean breeze felt almost alive, carrying with it the scent of a thousand sea creatures. "There is nothing more appealing to me than the smell of the ocean mixed with that of tropical flowers," I said to my friend. "It is in moments like this that you can feel and almost taste the connectedness of life." Flowers, some yellow and small, some big and red, feed the insects, who then feed the small fish, who are, in turn, eaten by the bigger fish, which ends up on our plate with a slice of lemon and a big red flower as decoration.

Unless viewed in terms of human survival, the economic value of conservation is sometimes difficult to demonstrate. Although the floating plants of the ocean, the microscopic phytoplankton, are of little direct economic value to people, and probably even less to economists, their elimination from the food chain would quickly destroy the world's marine fisheries, which are a major source of human food. In time, even the world's oxygen supply would be severely depleted. And, if you feel sorry for tiny marine life, what about the burning of the South American forests, the pollution of Eastern European rivers, the indiscriminate killing of gracious giant whales (those few left) in the Asian seas?

Much of the apparent conflict in the economics of conservation results from the difference between the greedy, short-term interests of small groups and the long-term interests of larger communities. The long-term economic benefits to be derived from stable and productive farmlands and forests are considerable when compared with the loss of farms that are exploited, eroded, and abandoned or forests that are cut, burned, and allowed to die. Short-term economic considerations are what lead individuals and communities to exploit their farms and forests for maximum profit at minimum cost and then move on, leaving the devastated lands behind.

Unfortunately, the green flag of conservation has been kidnapped by partisan political groups who focus media attention on selected issues (i.e., drilling in the Artic, an activity with very small negative impact on the environment), conveniently forgetting other much more devastating activities (burning of South American forests, colossal pollution of air, water and soil in Russia and China, systematic destruction of ocean life in Asian sea, etc., etc.).

Today, too many so-called economists focus their attention on the exploitation of what they believe are limited resources, while too few economists regard natural resources as a renewable part of the global system. While global warming goes on unchecked (most of the tropical glaciers from South America to Africa are melting at alarming rates, like Mount Kenya and Kilimanjaro, which have lost 80% of their ice caps, and even the mighty Himalayan glaciers are receding), few economists and business executives have expressed interest in the problem.

And, yet, most people would agree that natural resources should be treated as valuable and perpetual, in the sense of renewable components (if administered in responsible ways) of the global village, of "*spaceship earth,*" and always used for the greater good. And remembering one of the most famous spaceships: Star Trek's Enterprise, I'd like to borrow one of Mr. Spock's most famous lines: "Remember, the good of the many always comes before the good of the few . . . or the one."

If it is going to prosper, the future world economy must be based on responsible behavior, always placing the benefit of the whole community above the benefit of the single individual.

PAST VALUES

What must change?

In his last hours at the White House, President Bill Clinton pardoned a lot of criminals, and many on Wall Street hoped he would also pardon that anti-hero, crook-turned-do-gooder Michael Milken. Today, Michael is doing good work for charities and other worthy causes. In the 1980s, things were different, and Drexel-Lambert's Milken made hundreds of millions of dollars with junk bonds. That was the high point of the "Me" generation, at which time the book, *Secrets of Attila the Hun*, and its take-no-prisoners, conquer-and/or-destroy philosophy was the norm on Wall Street and in other financial centers. Were those values wrong?

Once upon a time, humans used to trade goods, often necessary goods, like food, clothing or tools. Later on, men started to use coins, gold, silver and all kinds of metal alloys. Then came the loans, the "I Owe You," and, worst of all, the borrowing by the State from its own people, the bonds, the promissory notes, and their un-natural offspring, the banks. Now we have credit cards, debit cards, and . . . Mr. Greenspan. But one of the most important things that need correcting in economics is the fact that past economic theories have been based on the wrong definition of what constitutes economic value.

This wrong interpretation of value has brought about materialistic theories, like Karl Marx's communist materialism, initiated with the publication of the infamous *Manifesto of the Communist Party* in 1848, but also by individualistic ones, like Adam Smith's capitalistic materialism (primarily from his book, *The Wealth of Nations*, published in 1798). One was more, the other a little less, but both theories are centered on the assumption that man's attitude is selfish and self-centered.

Today, it is necessary to replace the false assumptions of classical economics (scarcity of resources, ruthless law of natural selection [an anachronistic application of Darwin and Spencer's evolution theories], dialectical materialism, and other outdated economic ideas) with new and more empowering premises, such as the unlimited use of existing resources, the communal and social nature of men and women, and the hidden goodness of the human soul. And, even if Paul Romer's "ideas-based economy" is, in fact, part of the future, it is much too simplistic and certainly not sufficient to create a new, twenty-first century paradigm.

ROMEO AND JULIET

Like love, not all values need changing

Two households, both alike in dignity,
In fair Verona, where we lay our scene,
From ancient grudge break to new mutiny,
Where civil blood makes civil hands unclean.
From forth the fatal loins of these two foes
A pair of star-cross'd lovers take their life;
Whose misadventur'd piteous overthrows
Doth with their death bury their parents' strife.

Thus begins Shakespeare's tragedy and love epic of *Romeo and Juliet*. Montecchio is a small town, halfway between Verona and Vicenza, in the rolling, wine-producing hills of northern Italy. And, if you go there today, not much has changed since Romeo and Juliet's time.

You still find ancient houses, small winding streets, and ancient faces living ancient lives, with the same hopes, loves and dreams as their Shakespearian counterparts. And, today, like then, youthful, all consuming, hopeless, self-sacrificing love, like that of Juliet and her Romeo, lives on everywhere, from Verona to Brooklyn, from Kuwait City to Bombay. Love will never change.

In many situations, we see no limits to the willingness of men and women to bear untold "costs" in pursuit of certain invisible values, such as love, honor, truth, respect, and liberty, even at the cost of their lives. Even in our materialistic culture, most individuals have non-material desires and, therefore, find values that are non-material and non-monetary.

The fireman, the nurse, the preacher, the poet, the philosopher, and the artist all unite against cold economic "theories" and insist on the joy of giving without reward. It is creating for just the sake of creating, and they insist that human beings have the ability to find unlimited resources and creativity within themselves, often without need for reward or remuneration.

We all admire selfless and giving people like Mother Theresa of Calcutta. We enjoy Jimmy Stewart in movies like *It's a Wonderful Life*. We may cry reading Charles Dickens' *A Christmas Carol* because we all have some of that within ourselves.

The economist who does not expand his or her concept of value in the discussion of economics may be accused of "knowing the price of everything and the value of nothing." The business executive who tries to formulate a strategic plan without taking into consideration non-monetary factors and non-monetary values is destined, in the long run, to fail.

It is this commonality of purpose, these common characteristics, and this common nature that makes it possible, indeed necessary, to find our "common human denominator."

We should find the common values that are shared by all human beings, not because of their common traditions, but because of their identical inborn human nature, filled with their fundamental hopes, needs, and desires.

In recent times, Robert Heilbroner, an economist, and others have expressed their overall dissatisfaction with the superficial treatment of the concept of value by economists. Heilbroner writes, "I have gradually become convinced that the neglect of [the study of] value does not remove the issue from economics but only leads to its covert appearance in harmful form. I would venture that most economists today do not even see the need for a 'theory' of value, as distinct from a theory of price, and would in fact be hard pressed to explain the difference between the two."

Since the purpose of this book is to lay the foundation for the formulation of a globally acceptable theory of value and to stress its relevance in economy and in strategic and social planning, it focuses on the problem of *the source of value* (human desire, and not labor), and on the question of the purpose of human actions (value judgments and the process of valuation), not on a price theory. This is because it is necessary to first identify the sources of exchange value that underlie the external phenomena of prices, demand, and outputs in order to understand the process by which human factors and human values mold and structure human society and the economy.

If you think that this approach is too "philosophical" and not enough "economic," let's remember that both Adam Smith and Karl Marx were more philosophers than economists.

As strategic planning gains acknowledgement and acceptance (indeed "value") in corporate boardrooms the world over, it is important to also establish some unified standard, some set of acceptable rules by which to guide the decision-making process. Finally, economists need to develop a unified agenda for future dialogues and a set of criteria for the creation of an orderly, multi-valued, and globally acceptable world economy.

MARX AND MADONNA

We live in a material world

Madonna sold a lot of CDs a few years back with the hit song "Material Girl". And, like the song, many of us often feel like a material girl or boy. But there is a danger in being too materialistic. Historical materialism is the last, hardest-to-kill lie of Marxism-Leninism. You may not agree, but communism is not dead. Not yet. Marx is not dead in North Korea, not in Cuba, not in China, not in Italy or in France, not in many African and Asian nations, not even among some far-far-left individuals hiding in high and low places in every country of the world. But false values, like greed, self-centeredness, arrogance, the desire to dominate others, hypocrisy, and disregard for the well-being of the community or the environment can be the false virtues not only of communism, but also of a sick form of capitalism.

We can safely say that the national economies and economic dogmas of most countries on earth are founded on their predominant ideological traditions. And materialism (communism being its more destructive expression) represents an omnipresent reality in the entire western world and in much of the Orient as well; it is present in developed countries as well as in developing ones. All this, of course, inevitably affects the economy of each nation, and our economic system reflects this material sickness.

Do you love music? Could you live without music? Music and songs are everywhere, and not just found on the radio or on MTV and VH1. What about the music of birds, the ocean waves dancing on the beach, and the music of the animals in the forest or in the summer meadow? Is music more valuable than jewels?

An old story tells of the thief who stole some very valuable jewels and then ran into the desert to hide. In his haste, he forgot to bring enough water and bread. After days of painful wandering, a monk found the thief barely alive. "I'll trade you all my gold and precious stones for some bread and water," said the thief.

"Look at yourself," answered the monk. "You believed you knew what was important, and now those things have lost their value. You should learn to value those things that really matter."

What happened after that, I leave it to your imagination. What really matters is that we must find a better understanding of the way we perceive what is true value, which things are valuable and why, what things you can always carry with you, and what (like big gold bars on a sinking ship) you cannot (or you better not).

Throughout history, *idealism* and romantic ideals have often clashed with the pragmatic ideas of *materialism*. This has always been so. But, in recent years, the urge to make money at all costs has increasingly eliminated the former in favor of the latter. As an inevitable result, nearly all modern societies have returned to a morally barbarian state in which the values of liberty, spirituality and morality, even if given lip service by a few politicians, have certainly declined (and, in some cases, all but disappeared).

The nucleus of the family is also being violently attacked by the lack of ideals and the degeneration of ethical values and principles. These are some of the reasons for the Columbine High and other school shootings. Media moguls as well as politicians have a big responsibility in these changes. We must build our own future with a solid backbone and a fresh impulse to think, create and act on our own. In other words, we need a vision of what kind of world we want to have in the third millennium, what society and what inheritance we want to leave to our children. Do we really want to leave a huge hole in the ozone, fish full of mercury in the oceans, or societies centered on war and conflict?

The great capitalist countries have prospered until today by providing the material goods and comforts the masses craved, but now that's not enough. Activities, such as Greenpeace, environmental issues the world over, and the independence movements (Kurds, Albanians, and other ethnic groups) of people breaking free from ancient national barriers (Quebec, Scotland, Kashmir, Northern Ireland, Northern Italy, etc.) are demonstrating that we need more embracing goals and a new vision for the third millennium.

Democracy has one final obligation toward society, and that is to allow change and innovation to take place. If the free market system hasn't been able to stop the proliferation of drugs, pornography, family decadence, violence and crime, it means that this system must be improved, perhaps changed, in its core elements: its values and beliefs. With this book, I intend to simply indicate the direction in which such ideals can be found and developed. The war for economic supremacy is already in the works among the so-called great powers; it is, therefore, a priority to enter the new millennium with a better attitude and a more precise, peaceful, and wholesome global vision.

ROME

We need an empowering vision

It's a warm, mid-July morning in Rome. Imagine yourself sipping a tall cold drink at Café Canova in Piazza del Popolo. The scent of the olive-green Mediterranean pines blends with the perfume of the fresh bread and croissants baked a few hours earlier but still lingering in the air. The day is warm and sunny, the people easy-going, and the white and gray ruins of ancient Roman monuments give you a sense of continuity, like you yourself are part of that history. You feel relaxed, at home.

Rome is a city that catches your heart, if you let her. Look at the small restaurants in the old streets, the old fountains, and the bright orange sunsets. When you walk downtown, you feel like those ruins are alive. The ubiquitous stray cats, strolling or lying lazily around, look at you like past owners of those rundown, thousand-year old buildings. Did you know that one-third of the water used in present day Rome comes through ancient stone conduits, the aqueducts, built 2,000 years ago, at the time of Julius Caesar . . . and have never been repaired? The Coliseum could stand just as powerful as the one recreated in the movie *Gladiator,* if its statues and stones had not been pillaged during the last nineteen centuries.

So, what can we learn from past successes and past mistakes? In history, there have been innumerable lessons that have clearly shown how the lack of genuine, holistic values and a heartfelt public purpose have always brought about the stagnation and eventual fall of otherwise great civilizations.

The Roman Empire of two thousand years ago stagnated and fell because of the tragic subversion of its earlier empowering values by more selfish and decadent ones.

The loss of righteous values and its lack of vision and purpose were the real causes of its moral and cultural decay.

When the Roman Republic was young and had a vision of

its own destiny and place among other nations, it grew and prospered. With the transformation from Republic to Empire (around 40 B.C.), its leaders became more selfish, greedy and corrupted, and finally they lost that inspiring vision and those earlier, noble and empowering values. As a result, the Roman culture and civilization started to decay, and, without the power of Christian values and principles, it would have easily collapsed and disappeared like many other great civilizations before it.

Gradually, during the four centuries following the birth of Jesus of Nazareth, Christianity brought about a revolution in values, beliefs and vision. By so doing, Christianity provided the internal stimulus necessary to propel what was left of the old Roman Empire (and with it, most of Western civilization) to a new stage of development.

Before Roman times, the study of the problems of value, the creation and distribution of wealth, and other questions related to the economic and social life of society was being discussed as early as the beginnings of humanity. One of the most influential philosophers of Western civilization, Aristotle, provided, in the fourth century B.C., the foundations for a philosophical and systematic approach to the study of the concept of utility.

More than three hundred years before Jesus Christ, Aristotle, the great Greek philosopher, asked the question: "How is it that some of the most valuable things to life, such as air and water, are the least valued, while some of the least available ones, such as gold and precious stones, are so widely valued?" Aristotle's contribution to what we regard today as economics dealt in part with the exchange of commodities and the use of money, primarily from an ethical viewpoint.

Aristotle and his teacher, Plato, condemned the abuse of wealth and the "excessive satisfaction of unlimited desires and passions." Plato went so far as to prescribe limited personal property for the ruling political class. What a dreamer!

It was during the eight centuries after Socrates, Plato, and Aristotle that Western thought saw its greatest expansion, particularly through Roman civilization. *These early times witnessed the contribution of Roman law to the recognition of private property and the absolute respect for it*, laying the foundation for Western capitalism.

In New York's harbor, the Statue of Liberty holds two objects: the torch, the symbol of man's right to freedom, and a book of laws, that complementary tool without which freedom turns into chaos.

At the same time, *Roman law* granted respect for the freedom of the individual (if they were not slaves, of course), and *set the standard for the authority of the law over that of the rulers* (still followed in many nations . . . unless your name is Fidel Castro or Saddam Hussein). Roman humanities also increased the awareness of economic and social questions. Sometimes, I can't help but wonder what would have happened if Rome had embraced Jesus and his message while he was still alive.

ABRAHAM LINCOLN

An Enduring Vision

Eighteen centuries after the beginning of the fall of the mighty Roman Empire, a similar choice faced another great nation. A few years before the American Civil War, Abraham Lincoln delivered one of the most important and meaningful speeches of his career. The future President, giving his acceptance speech (on June 16, 1858) at the Republican State Convention in Springfield, Illinois, saw clearly that the nation had arrived at a major turning point.

Lincoln began: *"If we could first know where we are, and whither we are tending, we could then better judge what to do and how to do it."* Later on, he added: *" . . . agitation will not cease until a crisis shall have been reached, and passed. A house divided against itself cannot stand."*

The "house divided" quotation was one familiar to any church-going, Bible-reading citizen, as it is today. Lincoln understood and clearly communicated that slavery and freedom were incompatible, and provided, as on many other occasions in later years, an explicit vision of where the Nation should be headed.

By reviving healthy, Christian principles and values, turning away from self-centered and corrupting ways, Abraham Lincoln went on to become Senator, then President, bringing about the greatest positive change in American society.

Today, the values of freedom and slavery face each other on the global stage. After the terrorist attacks on the World Trade Center and the Pentagon, President George W. Bush held that: "The US will fight those with different values than ours," clearly drawing the line in the sand between freedom-loving cultures and repressive, isolationist, and enslaving (ask any Afghan woman) groups.

The difference between democratic values and the enslaving bent of different forms of dictatorships are well expressed in the words of Thomas Jefferson, when he wrote that: "The primary purpose of Government is to prevent harm to his citizens."

Islam is not the point of contention, rather, the real problem is the distorted interpretation of a few verses of the Q'uran that a few, power-hungry parties have used in order to con some of their more naïve and impressionable countrymen.

This is precisely the crux of the problem: different value systems. On one side, there are the values of life and liberty, freedom to worship (in any form), freedom to express one's ideas (free press), and freedom of assembly and petition (democracy). On the opposite side, the false values of fear and ignorance are used to secure the power to a handful of ruthless dictators, who use that fear and terror against their own people as well as against would-be enemies.

At this time, we do not need to stress cultural and religious differences, and mere tolerance is not sufficient anymore. What we need is to find the common points among different cultures and societies (my bet is that life and liberty are a good starting point) and, starting from them, build consensus and a brave new world (not an easy task, but easier if we know where we are and where we are going).

LEONARDO DA VINCI

We need to challenge old assumptions

I met Charles Dent on a clear spring day in the heart of the Pennsylvania countryside. It wasn't easy to find the "Dome," that unique artist's workshop and mini museum, where Charles was going to uncover his marvelous rendition of one of Leonardo Da Vinci's greatest unfinished works—the *Sforza's Horse*. Charles Dent was a passionate admirer of Leonardo, a sculptor, a wonderful human being and a great friend.

After many years of study, Charles produced what I consider to be the most exquisite reproduction of Leonardo's greatest sculpture, the *Sforza's* equestrian monument, an imposing and beautiful horse.

Today, thanks to the efforts of The Charles Dent Foundation and his longtime friend and associate, Roger Enlow, a thirty-foot high bronze of the "horse that Leonardo loved most" stands strong and majestic in Milan, Italy.

Today's arts and sciences are bringing to life a new twenty-first century Renaissance. The last Renaissance was four centuries ago.

The real significance of the scientific aspect of the European Renaissance, approximately from 1450 to 1700, was the transformation of many of society's fundamental assumptions, preconceptions, and beliefs by men like Galileo Galilei, Copernicus, Kepler, Christopher Columbus, and my very favorite: Leonardo Da Vinci.

The son of Sir Piero Da Vinci, Leonardo was born in Vinci, a small town twenty miles from Florence, Italy, in April 1452. The painter of the famous *Mona Lisa*, Leonardo grew up in the meditative hills of Tuscany and traveled and worked in Rome, Milan, and finally in France, where he died in 1519.

A true "master" in many disciplines, from sculpture and painting to architecture and engineering, *Leonardo's greatest strength was his willingness to challenge the dominant beliefs, the un-demonstrated notions, and the outright superstitions of his time,* placing him in the vanguard of one of the more profound cultural revolutions of western civilization.

Leonardo realized that, in order to change the old views (assumptions), one must first challenge one's own beliefs, cautioning that: *"The greatest deception men suffer is from their own opinions."* Today, in the middle of meaningful scientific, economic and cultural changes, we need to question and test our opinions and assumptions, even some of our beliefs and certainly some outright superstitions. We cannot remain shackled by outdated theories, deceived by ideological fallacies, or deluded by misconstrued and misplaced loyalties. We need new empowering ideas.

Marc Millis, a top scientist who works out of NASA's Glenn Research Center in Cleveland, is the head of NASA's Breakthrough Propulsion Physics Project. The Project is something that even the most forward-thinking rocket scientists have a hard time taking seriously—finding a propulsion drive or engine, a field generator, or other similar device that could help man travel to distant stars. When interviewed about his work, Millis said, "Are you familiar with the idea of out-of-the-box thinking? If you constrain yourself with what's possible, you'll work with what's already there. But, in the area of trying to go to the stars, that just won't hack it."

In the TV series, *Kung Fu*, the main character, when young, is reminded by his old blind master to question his own vision. "Remember, Grasshopper, sometimes even your own eyes deceive you."

Aren't we ever deceived by our own opinions? Remember the old joke: if you ass-u-me . . . you make an ass of you and me? Are our opinions and beliefs truly our own? Or do they mature under the constant fertilizing elements of the mass media, mass advertising and ideological propaganda? Do we own our ideas, our beliefs and values, or do they own us? And, are they really our own, or do we get them from our peers and society? Are we really free to change our minds and ourselves, if we want to, or are we slaves of what we have been told over and over again by the propaganda masters?

THE MATRIX

Today's answer

In the room, there were only a couple of old armchairs. Morpheus, the older man with the deep, reassuring voice, said to Neil, "The moment you questioned was the moment you chose your new destiny."

A few moments before, Trinity told Neil, "I, too, was looking for an answer. The question is what drives us."

In the meantime, deep down, into the bowels of the earth, people dream their computer-aided dreams, and the world, as we know it, goes on.

In the movie, *The Matrix*, a bit reminiscent of the novel *1984*, we find ourselves caught in a new yet age-old question: Is this reality that we perceive real, or is it just an illusion? Do we live in a dream, while the real world lies somewhere else, maybe closer to our dreams? To be or not to be? To dream or to awake? Are we really free or are we being deceived by something that manipulates our perceptions, our senses and our minds? What is the true nature of reality?

In Gerry Spence's book, *Give Me Freedom,* one feels some

of the same fear of the "corporate deception" and the repulsion for the hidden "masters" of our lives. Gerry Spence, the famous lawyer from Jackson Hole in Wyoming, starts his book with these words: "I ask you. Are you free? I say we are slaves. All of us."

Spence, who defines himself as a lawyer who spent most of his life representing the poor, the injured and the forgotten in the US Courts, believes, as many others do, that even in the land of the free, we are becoming more and more enslaved to a complex web of big corporate and big government monsters. Some of his stories are fantasy, others a little less so. The important thing is that men and women have often felt a loss of control over their own destinies.

"Alienation" was a big word in the 1960s psychology craze. Even Karl Marx, in 1848, spoke of alienation to vent his rebellious and revengeful nature and to justify the cult of class struggle and the destruction of the enemies of his deranged ideology.

We all know that, undoubtedly, things could be better. We could have a little more control over our situations, and we would like to a have a little more influence over "Big Government" or "Big Business." We could do more to protect our environment, have cleaner beaches and fresher air in our cities, enjoy more parking spaces downtown, and maybe even return to a little higher speed limit on our highways. Is it really that much to ask?

Matrix, the movie, had a nice subliminal message (maybe more than one!?!) about how to break the "code" that has kept people in darkness.

Are you one of the few who are ready to abandon the cozy, predictable, even sometimes hard life of your controlled sleep in order to face a more traumatic, maybe truer and possibly freer life?

The issue of control over one's own destiny is something we witness more and more, from life improvement seminars to movies.

Before presenting Neil with the choice of the two pills, the red or the blue, the choice to go on like before in ignorance, or to find out the hard reality, Morpheus asks his young friend, "Do you believe in Fate?" The answer, of course, is that most of us prefer to make our own choices. We prefer to be in control of our lives and of our immediate surroundings. But to what degree are we really free? Are our minds slaves to an invisible web of cleaver programs?

In his book on freedom, Gerry Spence goes on dreaming of "responsible corporations with a conscience" (employees, union and special interest groups on the Corporate Boards) becoming the valuable friends of man. "On the other hand," he continues, "the terror of continuing to live in a world in which these monsters rage out of control creates a nightmare from which we all must soon awaken or die in our sleep." But things may not be all that dramatic.

I believe that *the first, and maybe the only thing necessary to start freeing ourselves is to become aware of our own chains.* We need to understand the "matrix," the "code," and that means to understand what those chains are made of and how to remove them.

False beliefs, false values, corrupted laws, dark-age superstitions, unrealistic hopes, wrongful assumptions and misplaced traditions—these are the real villains.

Remember President Franklin D. Roosevelt's inauguration speech about "The only thing we have to fear is fear itself"? We should not be enslaved by fear. Fear is almost always the rotten manifestation of ignorance, and like rotting mildew and parasites, ignorance and fear grow in cold darkness.

Ignorance, the putrid feeding ground of fear, is, as many classic philosophers have argued since Socrates and Plato, the worst evil for man's mind, the most debilitating ill for man's body, and the saddest and most cruel pain for man's heart. I say, "Let's get rid of it all: fear, ignorance and despair, and smile at these powerless phantoms as they vanish completely in the sunlight, like undetectable mist in a hot summer morning."

END NOTES

Prehistoric notes

The natural world and our perception of it are such that they allow only a limited number of solutions to any given problem. Our prehistoric ancestors, be they hunters, fishermen, gatherers or farmers, if they wanted to survive in an often hostile environment, had to learn about realities relevant to their survival, by hunting, fishing, gathering, farming, or . . . stealing from other more successful villagers.

But, those of our prehistoric ancestors who did not contemplate survival-through-raiding techniques had to find the correct answers to questions such as: How do animals behave? How can they be captured or killed? Do they taste better roasted or raw? What tools are best suited to catch them? When and how must a seed be planted and how must it be nurtured in order to grow into fruits or vegetables? When is the right time to harvest? How can fire be started? Why is it not a good idea to start a fire in the middle of your field of wheat just before harvest time? Such experiences became part of the human heritage. This knowledge, formulated and accumulated through trial and error, became one of the most valuable things that an individual or a group could possess.

For a while, humans lived in an "information age" or "knowledge age," when the right kind of information was greatly valued—a little like today. But the "right" knowledge, in order to be truly valuable, must be valid in New York as well as in Albania. Take *pi* for example, the ratio of a circumference of a circle to its diameter. Everywhere in the world it is the same: 3.14 . . . etc. Anyone, regardless of his or her language and culture, who can draw a nice circle, measure its circumference and its diameter, and divide one by the other, will reach the same conclusion about the measure of *pi*. We all have the capacity to observe reality and, as a result, make up our minds about its meaning and decide how to act, but facts remain what they are, regardless of our opinion.

Years ago, an interesting movie (*Quest for Fire*) about prehistoric times and the quest for the making of fire was released in the theaters. I believe that primitive people must have had a somewhat mystical experience when they learned to tame and even create fire. Before that special moment, fire came from heaven, often in the form of lightning or a more rare volcanic eruption; sometimes, it came as the spontaneous combustion of dried grass on a hot summer day. But to our ignorant prehistoric ancestors, it must have manifested itself always as a supernatural force. Imagine the surprise of those people when someone learned to strike two rocks together and "miraculously" started a fire in the brush. There were many other mystical moments in our early history, like the discovery of the use of tools, as the famous movie, *2001: A Space Odyssey*, depicted so beautifully.

One single element has consistently served as the catalyst for human progress and evolution throughout the ages, and that is knowledge. From the day men learned to master fire and the wheel, to understand farming and onward, learning and knowledge have determined the advancement of the human race. But, real knowledge extends to all areas of human endeavor, like understanding the motion of the moon and other heavenly bodies, mathematical concepts, philosophy, economy, the nursing of the arts, understanding the human body and medicine, and, more recently, psychology and the study of the human mind and heart.

At this point, we could try to find a working definition of what is "value," a definition tied not only to man's desire for pleasure (as we will see further), but a more pragmatic definition tied to the pursuit of knowledge.

How is value created? Looking at value from a pragmatic viewpoint, we can see that value is created, among other things, by finding and sharing some kind of positive knowledge. By positive, I mean some kind of knowledge that can be put into practice, i.e., that can be translated into constructive action.

Let me add that also seemingly destructive knowledge, like

the discovery of gun powder for military use or the power unleashed by atomic and nuclear forces, can, and often does, further the progress of humankind. We can conclude that value is often found in the discovery and sharing of actionable knowledge. Naturally, this positive knowledge can enrich the individual seeking to fulfill his desire or pleasure, but it can also be found in a community context, that is, in actions or knowledge that benefit the whole society. When great knowledge is shared by great people, nations prosper.

From the Roman to the British Empire

Economics, in terms of monetary exchange, goes further back in time than the classical Greek and Roman philosophers. The origin of money as legal tender goes far back into the early history of humanity: in China from the 12th century B.C., in Lydia and the Middle East from the 14th century B.C.

It was only with the introduction of gold and silver that some unscrupulous soul found a way to shave some of the metal off the coins, so that the one-ounce gold coin that left the king's treasury returned two months later weighing about half of that. This illegal practice was universally condemned, and the debasement of money (today we call it inflation) became synonymous with depravity (even if, unfortunately, it does not seem so among some inflation-happy monetarists). Not before the late 15th and 16th centuries, with the introduction of merchants' banks, was the particular character and nature of "money" discovered, allowing a new economic age to begin.

The merchants emerged from Medieval times and became affluent. These entrepreneurs, who, in Medieval times, may have been called artisans, became not only wealthy, but also influential in both the political and cultural life of their respective countries. They influenced, to a great degree, the development of the age of the Renaissance.

The so-called modern state witnessed the conflict between the old feudal landowners, the land barons, and the new barons of trade (and, later on, of industry). The voyages of "discovery," such as those undertaken by Christopher Columbus in 1492, Vasco de Gama, Amerigo Vespucci, Clark, and others, revolutionized the "Old World" and, with it, its social status and values.

With the import of increasingly greater amounts of precious metals (particularly gold from the Americas to the ports of Portugal, Spain, and England) appeared one of the first well-documented increases in the price of commodities. The so-called great rise of prices, which was first documented by Jean Bodin (1530-1596), at first influenced the Spanish kingdom and, more particularly its port cities, where precious metals, spices, and other valuable commodities were unloaded from the new colonies.

From the 16th century on, the quantity of literature dedicated to the study of economics increased significantly, particularly in Western Europe. Most of these early writers were often businessmen who wrote pamphlets or treatises on a particular subject. Only in the 17th century do we see the beginning of the study of economics as an independent, intellectual discipline. Most of the body of literature of this period supported the principles and ideas of mercantilism.

According to Alexander Gray, in *The Development of Economic Doctrine*, "Mercantilism was anything but a system, it was primarily the product of the minds of statesmen, civil servants, and the financial and business leaders of the day." With the expansion of trade and voyages of discovery, merchant ships brought spices and other products from evermore-distant lands to their homeports. To cater to the merchants, banks appeared first in Italy (Venice and Genoa), then in France, England, Germany, and other European nations. Banks became one of the most influential institutions in the new life of Western civilization.

While the changing technology was having disruptive consequences on the old feudal order, it created an even greater challenge to the religious and spiritual life of Western Europe and its traditional values. The old scholastic notions of the virtuous life were so out of step with economic practices and scientific discoveries that the ethical and moral judgments of the churches became more and more inappropriate to the developing modern states. Individual activities became much less controlled by the old feudal landlords and by the churches because travel and increased communication allowed people a greater degree of individual freedom.

The production of art crafts and their delivery to the larger towns and emerging cities became more important than the ownership of land. Capital began to compete with land ownership, and the Industrial Revolution opened the doors to the new barons of industry (and countries supporting it, like England and Germany) and witnessed the decline of the great merchants and traders (in countries like Holland and the Italian States). New values, often more practical and materialistic, began supplanting the old ones. Since a wide diversity of views appeared in the economic and mercantilist literature between 1500 and 1750, it is difficult to analyze and concentrate on one topic. No single writer was really able to systematize his thoughts or his position until a more philosophical approach was brought to economic problems by the French thinkers—*les economistes*.

The french influence

The French contribution to the Age of Enlightenment cannot be overemphasized. The writings of Voltaire, Diderot, Condorcet, and Rousseau influenced much of our present-day scientific thought, and, also, to some extent, economic thought. The central role of agriculture to France and to its political economic thinkers made for an unusual development in the history of economic thought. The French economic thinkers of this time, trying to build a bridge between feudal times and the modern age, continued to regard agriculture, and, therefore, the ownership of land, as the main source of wealth.

The little-known school of physiocracy between 1750 and 1780 developed the first systematic approach to the study of economic questions. Its main advocate, Francois Quesnay (1694-1774), was the intellectual leader of a small group of students of the new field of economic thought. The physiocrats, just like the English economic thinkers, developed their economic theories in order to empower the government and the old landowning class with economic policies that were both correct and supportive of their political and societal systems. The physiocrats tried to approach economic theory from a "scientific" viewpoint. Their main concept was that of using natural law in the formulation of economic and social policies. Their belief that natural laws determined the operation of political economy brought them to believe that these laws were independent of human will, and that it could be possible to "discover" economic laws, just as their fellow scientists could discover the natural laws of physics, mathematics, and of the natural sciences.

The Scottish economist, Adam Smith, visited Paris in 1765 and, while criticizing the physiocrats' views on agriculture, paid respect to their academic achievements: "The agricultural system presently exists only of the speculation in a few men of great learning and ingenuity in France."

The physiocrats, or *les economistes*, as they referred to themselves, influenced the development of French economic and social policies for a considerable amount of time. François Quesnay was personal physician to Louis XV. One of Quesnay's disciples, Jacques Turgot (1727-1781), instituted tax and agricultural reforms, successfully at first, in the small town of Limoges.

Another of *les economistes* left France and established himself on the American continent. Pierre Samuel Du Pont de Nemours (1739-1817) left France right after the French Revolution and established one of the great business dynasties of the United States in Wilmington, Delaware.

Based on Rousseau's *Du Contrat Social (The Social Contract,* 1762), the French philosophers and theorists of the time developed the case against mercantilism and attacked the monopolies of the great trading houses in defense of the free market system and the emerging industrial class. The concept of *laissez-faire* and *laissez-passer* became one of the greatest legacies of the modern free enterprise and capitalistic system. Unfortunately, with it came the idea that wages should be held at the level of minimum necessity for subsistence.

In modern jargon, we could say that the major concern of the physiocrats was with the macroeconomic process of development. The physiocrats did not focus on money but on the physical forces leading to economic development. Partially in reaction to the mercantilist notion that wealth was created by the process of exchange, the physiocrats studied the creation of physical value and concluded (because of their biased motivation) that the origin of wealth was in nature itself, and more specifically, in agriculture.

Today, we witness a similar motivational bias when so-called economic experts and trend analysts attempt to explain and predict economic development. The disproportionate emphasis given to the information revolution and the excessive value ascribed to information technologies are creating a substantial distortion in the understanding of the real forces responsible for shaping human progress and for advancing scientific and economic standards.

The good, the bad, and the ugly: Adam Smith, Darwin, and Hobbes

There is no substitute for British humor, and if Thomas Hobbes had any sense of humor, he certainly did not share it with his readers. As early as the 17th century, English philosopher Hobbes (1588-1679) studied, among others, the works of Machiavelli (1469-1527), and expressed his concern about the consequences of materialism (even though he considered himself to be a skeptic and an anti-cleric). Hobbes wrote two works: *Leviathan,* to recommend a powerful secular state, and *The Elements of Law Natural and Politic,* as a defense to absolutism.

Hobbes believed that, in the future, nations would compete and fight ever more bitterly over increasingly rare natural resources, and mankind would end up in a fight of all against all, each individual desperately trying to snatch away from others the last bits of available goods.

Of course, Hobbes might feel he was right if he were to walk through the streets of present day Tirana, capital of Albania, or if he accompanied the Iraqi troops during their invasion of Kuwait. I am reminded of a wonderful book (*Eat the Rich* by PJ O'Rourke) I recently read about bad forms of capitalism and worse forms of socialism. Albania, Iraq and a host of third world countries show exactly what happens to a free market when there is no legal, political, or traditional framework to limit freedoms and to protect marketplaces. Of course, there's lots of violence, as you'd expect in a situation where the shopkeepers and the shoplifters have the same status under their so-called laws, and where often the police protects their own interests before protecting yours. And, of course, there's lots of poverty.

As O'Rourke mockingly points out, theft is the opposite of creating wealth. Instead of adding value to assets through hard work, creating wealth by increasing the value of things, theft moves assets from higher-valued uses to a fence who, if you are lucky, pays five cents on the dollar for them. But capitalism conducted in a condition of anarchy also produces some less-predictable results, like today's Russia, where the mafia, the KGB, the businessmen and the politicians sometimes share the same bed . . . or the same name.

Now that some of the centralized and stiff economical systems of the former communist block have been dismantled, the battle for the conquest of those markets is just beginning. The *arms race* has been replaced by a *race to virgin markets*, but the morality of those involved and the methods used to acquire such markets are very much questionable. Former communist governments should try to regulate such scramble to the booty in order to protect the public interests, as well as those of consumers and workers. Also, the economic cracks in the majority of Asia's financial markets ought to have people reflecting on the dangers of a deregulated situation. According to Hobbes, by now the entire world would be an exceedingly hostile and competitive environment.[1]

Looking at the relatively healthy state of the American economy (in spite of Mr. Greenspan's efforts to weaken it), we can feel relatively distant from that tragic scenario. Revolutionizing entirely the thesis of his predecessors, Hobbes defined as a "natural right" the individual's egotistic claim to enjoy the greatest possible amount of goods.

Today, some similar humor can be found in the works of Jeffrey Sacks. According to Sacks, Harvard scholar and former economic advisor to the governments of Poland and Hungary, the economic future is to be found in a kind of 19th century American West form of capitalism. He is convinced that the only possible answer to the problems of the former Communist countries is *"a free, deregulated economy, a large private enterprise and a unruled market; also, the demand for a redistribution of the land in the former Warsaw Pact nations should be denied in the name of equality."* Such statements could be the material for Comedy Club jokes (if they weren't taken so absurdly seriously by so many economically desperate leaders of former socialist nations). Nothing can be more un-righteous, in my opinion, than to deny to the people the land stolen by Communist regimes in the past 80 years. Fortunately, some Russian figures have spoken out on this issue. Those millions deprived of government jobs, including the once formidable Soviet military, should be allowed to colonize sections of the land, as it was done during the American westward expansion.

Another way-too-overrated economist is Francis Fukuyama, whose *The End Of History* doesn't base itself on any kind of value theory. *Liberal democracy* and liberal economy will be, according to Fukuyama, the rule of the future. Fukuyama suggests that capitalism is the answer to past, present and future social problems. But, at this point, we have to remind him and his superficial admirers that several major wars, including the two World Wars, spawned from capitalistic countries. In this respect, Edward Luttwak, an international consultant, strategist and writer, provides, in his latest book, *Turbo Capitalism*, no real solutions but describes more precisely and in powerful details the economic changes taking place in the world.

In fact, the race to economic power can be just as dangerous as the race to military or ideological supremacy. Fukuyama also throws in opinions about European nationalism that he defines as *"dead, beaten and deprived of any weight in world's politics."* That is also a very wrong assumption, devoid of any factual observation. (Maybe he should also spend a few days in Albania and see the results of extreme forms of economic liberalism or ask the people of Kosovo and Serbia about European nationalism.) Economic history is not at its end, rather, it has arrived at a turning point. Global economics can only work if we recognize the connective reality of a networked global society and act as responsible stewards of our planetary home and neighbors.

Adam Smith

From the Industrial Revolution emerged two great, yet conflicting systems of thought, two political economies. The first supports what today we call "capitalism" and is based on the work of Adam Smith. About a century later, the second, centered on Karl Marx's *Das Kapital,* spawned socialism and communism. Adam Smith was among the first of a small group of writers whom we call today the "classical economists."

The classical period in economics extended approximately from the second half of the 18th century to the end of the 19th. The major writers of this period were Smith, David Ricardo, John Stuart Mill, and, in a field of his own, Karl Marx. Some of the precursors and thinkers who more directly influenced the thought and writings of Smith were David Hume, the English philosopher (1711-1776), and the physiocrats, particularly Quesnay. Modern economists have hailed Smith as the practical forefather of modern capitalism. John Kenneth Galbraith called Smith "the prophet of the new economic order."

Born in 1723, near Edinburgh, Scotland, Smith became a professor of Moral Philosophy at Glasgow University. Smith's beginnings as a philosopher can be clearly detected in his book, *The Theory of Moral Sentiments* (1759), which preceded his major work, *An Inquiry into the Nature and Causes of the Wealth of Nations* (1776). Thus, Smith did not begin his career as an economist but rather as a humanist. There is no question that Smith was largely influenced by his teacher, Francis Hutcheson (1694-1746), and by the writings of Hume. Smith shared with Hutcheson a basic disapproval of the mercantilist position in reference to money and currencies. Because of his background in moral philosophy, Smith based most of his wide-ranging work on the basic assumption that human beings are driven primarily by their egoistic or self-centered nature. Smith's methodology has been generally described as a form of the deductive method mixed with historical and institutional descriptions.

Adam Smith witnessed an age of great transformation. The static order that characterized the late Middle Ages was being completely supplanted by a period of great changes, challenges, and revolutions. The changing environment, brought about by the ideas of the Reformation, the newly re-discovered human values of the Renaissance, and the practical applications of the Industrial Revolution, contained the seeds for the new economic order (and new values which were justified by Adam Smith and the so-called classical political economists).

In some of his travels through Europe, Smith is said to have visited Voltaire in Geneva (Switzerland) and Quesnay and Turgot in Paris. Smith brought back with him from the continent a sense of the new discipline of political economy and an understanding of the need, on the part of the ruling class, to find ways to organize and direct the new economic powers being created.

Smith addressed not only an audience that was ready to receive his message, but also a growing capitalist class eager to be justified in their economic behavior. The new nation-states were looking for "scientific" theories that could justify their policies of self-interest. A new set of values and principles was emerging, and it was necessary to find a systemic approach to explain and justify those new values and the new vision of the world and the world to come. As the cities grew, the increased productivity of agriculture simultaneously provided the elements necessary for the creation of new industries and the growth of factories and plants.

Following the Reformation, particularly in Germany and later in France and England, the scholastic views tied to the religious views of the Roman Catholic Church were being gradually and inexorably replaced by the Protestant worldview, the "Protestant work ethic" and the Protestant view of "equality." When the printing press made the Bible available to whoever could read, the monopoly of the Scriptures (held by the Roman Catholic Church for centuries) crumbled, and scores of new and unauthorized interpretations of the Biblical message mirrored the new emerging values of the changing European societies.

Of fundamental interest to the traders and the mercantilists was the determination of the most effective ways to increase the wealth of a nation. Even though some of the new economic problems concerning the distribution of wealth had already appeared, this problem was not brought to the forefront until later in the nineteenth century. Overall, the changing trend of religious thought brought about a noticeable change in the economic activities within it. The teachings of John Calvin (1509-1564) and his followers (first in Geneva and then in most of Western Europe) were not only compatible with the new economic activity, but, according to Max Weber and RH Tawney, contributed directly to the rise of the capitalist system.

Smith could be defined today as a macro-theorist particularly interested in the elements determining the economic growth of the nation. Smith's scope in his major book, *The Wealth of Nations*, followed that of English mercantilists and French economists. Even if Smith cannot be defined as an economist in the narrow sense of the word, his greatest strength lies in his vision and ability to correlate different segments of the study of economics with his knowledge of the historical economic trends available to him.

Smith was certainly more philosopher than economist in the

contemporary sense of the word, but one who was pointing the way to economic development and progress. Together with the mercantilists, Smith shared the ideas, very common in his time, that through the development of the physical sciences, it was possible to discover the so-called laws of economy.

The scientific method of investigation led many thinkers to believe that it was possible to discover the relationship between cause and effect, not only in the hard sciences but also in the problems dealing with society and human nature. One of the other assumptions that we find in Smith and later political economists is that human beings are both rational and calculating, and that their primary aim is economic self-interest. One difference between Smith's assumptions and that of most mercantilists was that Smith thought competitive markets did exist, and that the factors of production move freely within these markets to take economic advantage. Another important assumption was that Smith believed in the existence of some sort of natural force, an invisible hand, which works in the economic area and can resolve economic conflicts more efficiently than any arrangement devised by humans.

In the words of Smith:

> As every individual, therefore, endeavors as much as he can to employ his capital in the support of domestic industry and so to direct that industry that its produce may be of the greatest value, every individual necessarily labors to render the annual revenue of the society as great as he can. He generally, indeed, neither intends to promote the public interest, nor knows how much he is promoting it. By preferring the support of domestic to that of foreign industry, he intends only his own security; and by directing that industry in such a manner as its produce may be of the greatest value, he intends only his own gain, and he is in this, as in many other cases, led by an invisible hand to promote an end which was no part of his intention.[2]

In other words, the basic assumptions, which today we would call a paradigm, from which Smith develops his theories, consist of the following beliefs:

1. Humans are rational and calculating beings,
2. Humans are driven primarily by self-interest, and
3. When allowed to develop and compete freely, this self-interest automatically promotes the interests of the whole society in which the individual exists.

From these premises, Smith concluded that governments should not interfere in the economic and industrial process and should, therefore, follow a policy of free enterprise, the same laissez-faire and laissez-passer to which both the mercantilists and the French economists subscribed (though for different reasons). Throughout his works, we notice Smith's desire to prove that private ownership and self-interest, when expressed in an unregulated market economy, will lead necessarily to the greater public good.[3]

According to Smith, motivation is one of the primary assumptions and primary forces moving the economic machine. Economic motivation, for Smith, is based almost entirely on self-interest. One of Smith's famous quotes says: "It is not from [other people's] benevolence . . . that we expect our dinner, but from their regard to their own interest. We address ourselves, not to their humanity, but to their self-love."[4] Smith, later on, added that, "I have never known much good done by those who affected to trade for the public good. It is an affectation, indeed, not very common among merchants, and very few words need be employed in dissuading them from it."[5]

Probably the most revolutionary step that Smith took in his political economy was to depart radically from the morals of religious philosophy by rejecting the notion of self-interest as sinful. He found no element denoting a sinful behavior anywhere in human self-interest, rather, he identified that it was that very force which was thrusting the society toward betterment and progress. Through the "invisible hand," self-interest had become a public benefactor. One of the reasons Smith's message became so popular was, without question or doubt, because he addressed an audience that was certainly ready to receive it. The growing capitalist class was eager to be justified in its activities. The new nation-states were looking for a philosophy that would justify their policies of self-interest and expansionism. This justification of the "natural greed" in humans served also many individuals' personal inclinations, and it so continues in our own time.

Even today, in the chambers of commerce around the world, in the financial centers of New York, London, Tokyo, and Hong Kong, the justification for human self-interest is accepted as the underlying assumption for any public policy and action. Today, economic "survival of the fittest" rules economies, both in the so-called developed and developing countries. While self-interest may clearly represent the primary force motivating the butcher and the baker, the justification of self-interest at the national and international levels can only bring about wars and conflicts.

Smith's work favored the overcoming of the value of tradition, the old "credence," by the new values of independence, self-worth, self-improvement, just like Martin Luther, a few centuries earlier, preached a sort of "self-salvation," following a long tradition going back to the legend of King Arthur and the celebration of the victory of the individual (the King of humble birth) over the old tradition and the old aristocracy (brought to fruition in the American, 1776, and French, 1789, Revolutions).

Today, capitalist societies, as well as the former communist societies, are being reduced to an economic war of each against all. Everyone seems to be struggling for self-preservation in a world that would have made Charles Darwin and Herbert Spencer proud of their evolutionary theories and their "survival of the fittest" mindsets. At the societal level, self-interest is most obviously not the instrument of an "invisible hand." Rather, as Socrates told his disciple, Plato, " . . . all wars are undertaken for the acquisition of wealth."[6] Similarly today, Paul Kennedy, in his book, *The Rise and Fall of the Great Powers*, tells us that the defense systems of nations are in place mainly for the protection of wealth.[7]

In the very first paragraph of *The Wealth of Nations*, Smith presents his argument that the nature of the wealth of nations is determined not by the accumulation of precious metals (gold), as the mercantilists stated, but rather by the productivity of labor.

> *"The annual labor of every nation is the fund which originally supplies it with all the necessities and conveniences of life which it annually consumes, and which consists always either in the immediate produce of that labor, or in what is purchased with that produce from another nation."* [8]

But, while at the beginning of his work, Smith suggests that it is the annual labor of every nation that brings about its wealth, in the latter part of his work, it is possible to note a change of position and certain confusion. The productivity of labor somehow mutates into the accumulation of capital. At first, the productivity of labor increases through the specialization and division of labor, but, later, this theory of the productivity of labor as the primary force of the wealth of a nation gradually changes into an increase of capital formation. First, Smith tells us that the wealth of a nation depends upon the productivity of labor (this would make most Chinese communists very happy) and the proportion of laborers who are usefully or productively employed. He also suggests that the wealth of a nation should be measured in per capita terms. Today, we agree that, when we say that England is wealthier than India, it is understood that the comparison is not based on total GNP or total output of the two countries, but on per capita income of the population.

In Smith's own words:

> *"The annual produce of the land and labor of*

any nation can be increased in its value by no other means, but by increasing either the number of its productive laborers, or the productive powers of those laborers who had before been employed. The number of its productive laborers, it is evident, can never be much increased, but in consequence of an increase of capital, or of the funds destined for maintaining them. The productive powers of the same number of laborers cannot be increased, but in consequence either of some addition and improvement to those machines and instruments which facilitate and abridge labor, or of a more proper division and distribution of employment. In either case an addition of capital is almost always required." [9]

The result of this type of reasoning is that capital is, even more than labor and the division of labor, the main cause and goal of the wealth of nations (and this conclusion makes us, in the Western world, very happy, too). The enormous impact that these conclusions have had on the economic policies of Western society cannot be overemphasized. Smith defended the laissez-faire, laissez-passer policy, arguing that the accumulation of capital could only develop in an institutional framework of free markets and private property. The laissez-faire policy, he thought, would assure that capital would be accumulated and then allocated so as to insure the highest rate of economic growth. The impact of these conclusions on economic policy in the industrialized world, from the United States to Japan, has been and continues to be extremely important.

The end of the 20th Century is witnessing another important transition from the Information Age to what I call the "AGE OF LIBERTY AND WISDOM." Already, the most innovative minds are developing the idea of an ongoing transition from the information era and the supremacy of information technology to a more advanced stage of development, with the ability to create new, more effective and efficient products, processes and systems determining the value of an individual, a team, or an organization.

Acting as a consultant to some of the major political parties in Italy, like Forza Italia and the Northern League, I have been fighting (with millions of other Italians) for a greater degree of freedom in the economic life of that nation. It is my firm belief that the next decades will witness a great increase in the value ascribed to creative ability, and that greater value will be given to systems and environments that allow a greater degree of freedom, thus stimulating individual and group creativity.

Unfortunately, some of the political and economic alliances made right after World War II have been weakened by several unexpected facts, such as: 1. The decline of America as a moral and social point of reference, 2. The ascension of new markets and political/economic powers, such as those in the Orient, in South America, and in the Arab peninsula, 3. The seeming demise of Soviet Communism (but not all its other forms), 4. The partial unification of Western Europe and the birth of several other new alliances worldwide, and 5. The coming of age of the Islamic world.

The American media have attributed an excessive importance to the rise of Japan as an economic power and to the building of what has been called the "European fortress." *The real problem of the United States*, however, lies not in the competition for capital nor in the competition to which American-made products are exposed, but rather in *the loss of its own identity as a moral and ethical nation* based on the human and ethical values that helped making it strong in the first place.

There is a vivid danger that without such value and guidance, the leading class of America might just lead the country on a rocky and aimless road, full of peril and riddled with decadence, as the many scandals of the Clinton era have demonstrated. At this point, a review and a renewal of its own ethical, moral and social pillars (and not just the religious ones) should be a priority not only for America, but also for the rest of the world.

Darwin, Spencer and the Jungle

Don't misunderstand me. I have always loved movies like Walt Disney's *Tarzan* or *George of the Jungle*. I practically forced my kids to see them with me. But, I detest the way greedy businessmen and superficial economists try to use Darwin's and Spencer's theories of the so-called law of the jungle and survival of the fittest to justify some businesses' reprehensible and sometimes criminal behavior.

Darwin was not a philosopher, and we could say that he was glad to let others draw the philosophical construct out of his own so-called scientific investigations. Darwin hardly used the term "evolution" and never dealt directly with the development of human beings. On the contrary, he was careful not to deal with anything but animal species. Even before Darwin, the idea of evolution had been already discussed for some time, but it was his book, published in 1859, on the *"Origin of Species by means of natural selection, or the preservation of favored races, the struggle for life"* that gave the idea of evolution its greatest burst. In *Origin,* Darwin gave his theories a systematic form immersed in an ocean of observable facts.

Herbert Spencer (1820-1903), a disciple of Darwin, professed to be a scientific philosopher and regarded the scientific method as the best approach to human knowledge. It was Spencer, in his *System of Synthetic Philosophy*, who tried to provide a grand, speculative explanation of the entire natural world, the descent of man included. Spencer's total approach is not only naturalistic, but, most important, it is materialistic (Hobbes) and, to a smaller degree, positivistic (Comte and Mills).

But, unlike Mills and other British thinkers taken by the false promises of socialist propaganda, Spencer considered socialism a by-product of the militaristic, feudal society, as it later showed itself to be. Darwin and Spencer were both influenced by Malthus' terrifying prophecies. Too often, the Darwinian theories of the *law of the jungle* and the *survival of the fittest* (these expressions were actually coined by Herbert Spencer) have been used by speculators, businessmen of all sorts, and careless economists, all eager to justify their unorthodox tools and practices. It would certainly be good to carefully study such methods, analyze them from various points of view, and try to understand the reasons for their appearance, so as to be able to replace them with methods more compatible with human dignity and integrity. This work I leave to more ethically minded authors.

Again, let me state that I am not opposed to evolution theories; on the contrary, there is enough evidence of biological evolution, but the history of economies does not bear witness to any kind of "economic evolution." The only consistent fact is that communities all over the world have always stressed the need to improve their living conditions, their educational standards, and the preservation of their environment, often asking for a strong and stable political leadership. Unfortunately, not too many politicians and even fewer economists have ever been able to provide the necessary leadership to effectively meet these challenges.

Critique of some economic assumptions

Today, there is some confusion over the concept of economic value. Part of this confusion is attributable to economic value theories having inadequate grounding in axiology (the study of value). It is imperative that a new, strategically organized value system, one grounded in an original and systematic view of man, arises to resolve these and other problems if we are to arrive at a workable and globally acceptable economic theory and a new "matrix." Partly in response to logical positivism's belief that the purpose of science is to establish "the truth," Thomas Kuhn, in *The Structure of Scientific Revolution (1962)*, wrestled logical positivists' methodology by introducing the concept of the "paradigm." Paradigm is the "in-born" approach built in the researchers' worldview, an accepted set of beliefs that would remain as part of any "scientific work" until discrepancies are discovered due to new data, which would create the need for a superior paradigm, thus creating the emergence of a new scientific revolution. To use religious terminology, the search for truth has its "fundamentalists" (logical positivists), and the believers in the "on-going revelation", such as Thomas Kuhn and his "paradigmatic" belief that, while a superior truth (theory) might exist, it may remain unpopular (even heretic) because of the society's inertia in favoring the old paradigm. Kuhn viewed an ever-increasing body of "truths" sometimes kept back by society's resistance to change and by various interest groups favoring the old, existing paradigm. This and other works showed that the basic assumptions preceding any theory or hypothesis (the paradigm) influence the type of "truth" discovered.

The problem of self-centeredness

Self-centered and individualistic approaches breed conflict and stagnation (and excessive greed, as in the case of Enron and friends, may also bring jail sentences), while holistic and community-serving approaches to economic activity bring about synergistic energies. There is a tendency in human beings, often discouraged in business practices, to share one's abilities with others, which brings about the best in people. Largent and Breton, two writers searching for moral economic principles, say it best: "Cross-pollinating our creative abilities makes economic exchange synergetic. Through exchange, diversity increases diversity. Knowledge, skill, and creativity feed each other to yield possibilities greater than what individuals alone could produce."[10]

Money is not the only possible measure of value, and to try to reduce every thing and every human activity to monetary (and thus numeric) values limits greatly the economic horizon and distorts reality to a point that goes below the most basic function of human nature.

Mankind has proven, throughout the ages, that it doesn't know any limits to creativity, and, while some economists try to convince us of our shortcomings and limitations, it would be helpful to remember that human talent, creativity, adaptability, and courage (risk-taking) in the face of adversity have (eventually) always won over limitations, restrictions, oppression, and fear.

The famous historian, Arnold Toyenbee, has eloquently presented the cycle of the rise and fall of civilization, and the ability of man to rise to increasingly more difficult challenges.[11] Economic theory and investigation are better served if we abandon this archaic view, selfish attitude, and invalid assumption of the "law of the jungle" and of the "survival of the fittest."

Closely connected with the issue of a "self-centered" and "self-limiting" type of thinking is the assumption (widespread in economic thought) of the scarcity of resources.

The problem of assumed scarcity

Scarcity of resources—what nonsense! It reminds me of the example of the blind man who died of starvation in the middle of a banana plantation. To manage resources, economists try to take stock of what is readily available. From the days of Thomas Malthus, Adam Smith, and David Ricardo, most economic theories have assumed the scarcity of resources. Most of us have come to agree, without questioning it, that world resources must be limited.

To Malthus and a few of his modern followers, such as the Club of Rome and other more or less deranged minds, overpopulation and the scarcity of tillable land seem so dangerous that wars and other "plagues" may be viewed as possible "solutions" to the problem. While it is true that there are several important limitations to the availability of certain material resources, it is equally true that human creativity and adaptability seem to be limitless.

It has been said that assuming scarcity in every aspect of economic life is like assuming that the limited number of (chemical) elements limits chemistry, or that the limited number of notes limits music. Go tell that to Wolfgang Amadeus Mozart! Breton and Largent, in their delightful book, *The Soul of Economies,* remind the reader that: *"Nor are the best symphonies those with the most notes. The value of each lies in their ingenious arrangement. So, too, in economies: arrangements introduce order. Order multiplies the way we use our resources and so (it) functions as an anti-scarcity factor. With order, we can do more with less, not by skimping but by being creative."*[12]

We must know that the assumption of scarce resources can be challenged, as it has been in the last decades, by new technological and scientific advances. Some of the readers may remember the long lines at the gas pump during the so called "oil crisis" of 1974. We may even wonder if, in the 1970s, the obsession with oil as the "only available" energy resource was derived from an acute case of economic myopia, or if it was presented and "packaged" in a certain way for the general public by certain special interest groups.

Quite often, before elections, people question the government about the lack of research in alternate energy sources, but, a few months after each election, everyone forgets their questions and the world goes on as usual, relying on fossil fuels, filling the air with millions of metric tons of carbon dioxide and other poisonous gases, and creating increasingly difficult pollution problems. Kenneth Boulding focuses on this problem when he says that: *"The whole theory of value in economy assumes scarcity. Suppose, however that the society is so affluent or its desires so undeveloped that everyone has what he or she wants. Under these conditions the whole theory collapses."*[13]

Peter Drucker, one of the innovators of management science, wrote that: *"The source of wealth is something specifically human: knowledge. If we apply knowledge to tasks we already know how to do, we call it 'productivity'. If we apply knowledge to tasks that are new and different, we call it 'innovation'. Only knowledge allows us to achieve those two goals."*

Because one of the greatest challenges facing regional economic unity is the problem of harmonizing conflicting economic interests, it is imperative that the public and private sector meet to develop the formulation of a globally acceptable system of values and principles (one that would provide guidelines for the evaluation of the direction that both economies and society are taking) in order to share common goals (centered on mutual benefits and benefits for the environment) and, particularly, a common vision for the future.

CHAPTER II

BIRTH: ME, MYSELF, AND ALL THE OTHER STUFF

A Binary concept rules the human mind: Me and the World

It was late night, about 3:00 am. There was a full moon. I was in Utah on Highway 80 in the vast, almost limitless expanse of the Great Salt Lake, a few miles off the Rocky Mountains. I was driving to Oregon, when I felt the urge to stop on that desert highway and walk on that prehistoric salt.

I found myself alone, on the limitless, white, salty, plain, with no sounds and no wind, above me only the embracing blanket of the warm night sky. While the ancient, hard, salt cracked under my feet, the milky full moon seemed to reflect the white desert and the ancient, water-sculptured rocks. Few other times have I felt so alone. And yet, I was filled with the presence of everything around me. But, above and among all things ruled a filling awareness of my own "Self."

We have all had these moments. John, a former editor of the Miami Herald and an old friend of mine, experiences that sense of oneness with his own Self in the quiet of a morning walk. Others may feel something similar listening to music, dancing, driving at night on empty highways, reading, painting, working, playing sports, or writing deep, personal thoughts on snowy sheets of paper.

The Self—no word can describe it. We alone know our own Self; we alone experience it from the moment of our birth. We are born as "Self." Then, some time later, from the moment we become aware of "others," we understand that this type of "reality-of-the-Self" is not limited to ourselves, but that all people possess their own unique, individual Self, yet we are the only ones to really know our very own Self.

The day of our birth is certainly one of the most important events in our lives . . . you can't argue with that! From the very moment we come out screaming in this cold and crazy world, we immediately establish a fundamental distinction between "ME" and "everything else out there."

After screaming for air, screaming for food, screaming to be cleaned, and after resting from all the screaming, the baby looks around. If lucky, he or she will gaze at a mother's loving face. If less lucky, the baby may stare at the blinding, fluorescent lights and formless white ceiling of the maternity ward, while listening to the other newborns still screaming.

Eventually, we all observe the world out there and start, unconsciously, to systematize what we observe and what we experience according to a binary, relational lattice.

Thus, the first things we perceive fall into two categories: 1. What's good for me, and 2. All the rest. "Mother's-milk: good." "Gentle-rocking: good." "All-other-babies-screaming: gives me a bad headache." "Doctor-who-spanked-me: no-good." "Nice-looking-nurse-who-changes-my-diapers: good" . . . well, maybe not that early. Anyway, you get my point.

So we systematize two very different concepts: 1. The Self

(both our body and our inner awareness): *the one*, and 2. All other things outside of ourselves: *the many.*

First, the baby tends to perceive other objects through taste (mother's milk) and then visually (picking objects and tasting them). Then, measuring distances through vision and touch, he or she perceives space. Later on, with the repetition of some activities (like feeding) and the observation of motion and movement, surfaces the notion of time.

What really goes on in the baby's mind, I do not know. But what's important are the common, binary, basic concepts that form in our minds at this early stage, and these are: *1. Me (the Self), and 2. All other things.*

Me and the world are not just two ideas, but two separate realities (two very separate entities) interacting in a multi-variety of sense-perceptions, sometimes clashing, other times dependent, almost always connected.

We could say that, in order to organize our perception of reality, we create a binary scaffold. This "me-world" becomes a kind of binary lattice upon which we develop all other concepts. This binary matrix determines all other perceptions and may even influence our perception of reality as being somehow symmetrical.

Observing the learning process of a child, we see that most of our fundamental concepts and ideas can be reduced to our perception of those two types of reality: the Self and the World.

There is no doubt, and if you want you can read all the boring supporting material in the endnotes, that the most fundamental and the most elemental distinction in our mind is between the concept of "ME, the all-important "SELF" on one side, and "THE WORLD," every *other* thing, on the other side. Why and where this type of organization comes from, I cannot tell you. Maybe it springs from our DNA, from the form of the "double helix" of our genes. Maybe it comes from the form of our two-sided brain. Others will figure it out. *What really matters is the basic binary distinction between "Me" and "The World".*

But the "one" and the "many" form no static contradistinction.

There is rather, a moving, energizing complement as well as a dialectical tension between them. The history of religions shows various efforts to combine unity and multiplicity in the conception of the divine. Is it two realities or two sides of the same coin? I do not care to enter into what I consider metaphysics. It is enough for now to have established the beginning of our journey into the way we perceive reality.

Human beings systematize their perceptions starting from this most basic binary concept: myself-others, me-world, one-many.

PERSONAL PERCEPTIONS

Encoded knowledge

A few days after birth, we get the idea that the world is a lot more complicated than what we expected, certainly less comfortable than the watery womb that secured us for the last nine months or so. To make sense of this chaotic situation, once we have distinguished the new reality "out-there" from our self-identity "in-here," we start to organize our perceptions in such a way as to categorize the new inputs.

This framework of perceptions, some sensual and some mental, becomes the foundation upon which we judge our experiences, good and bad. *We use the matrix as a kind of template, a mental operating system, to organize what would otherwise be a storm of chaotic data.*

There is a Russian saying that everyone looks at the world from the bell tower of his own village. Perceptions differ because our experiences differ and because we choose and select from among our experiences. Each one of us observes and interprets different types of data, in part, because we are all interested in different things.

Depending on our specific perspective, our perceptions vary. Most humans and a host of other sentient beings learn not only from experience, but also by imitating successful behaviors. A baby bear, a baby tiger, and most other babies learn to survive by following and imitating their parents, but, before that, we all need a scaffold, a matrix, an operating platform upon which to write all new information.

Before even the most basic learning can begin, we need an organizing system. So we develop a binary, or, better yet, a relational system, according to which way we sort and arrange present and past experiences. Our perception of reality begins as a bi-polar relationship: "myself-world" or "myself-others" or "one-many."

Based on our perspective, we also selectively view additional information. We tend to collect evidence that supports our prior views and to dismiss or ignore nonconforming data. This screening process has at least three levels: 1. We selectively remember what we want to, 2. We selectively recall what we remember, and 3. We revise our memories to fit our preferences. The more we become convinced of our views, the more we filter out information that would lead us to question them. In reading a newspaper, each of us is likely to skim many stories while noting one in particular that confirms a prior view: "See that? Just what I expected."

But be careful, to the extent that our current perceptions are distorted, our future perceptions are likely to become even more so. The more entrenched our partisan perceptions become, the more obvious it is to us that we are right and others are wrong. Terrorists are seen as freedom fighters by those who would like to be free. Freedom fighters are seen as terrorists by those who are terrorized. Teenagers, sometimes viewed as terrorists by some folks for choosing models that do not necessarily inspire them to bring up their more positive and creative potential, often see themselves as fighters for their own freedom. Personally, I love teenagers. They are so ready to challenge any old idea, any unproven dogma, every boring tradition.

THE KEY TO VALUE

Perception

We all come into the world in the same way: we are born as small, screaming creatures unaware of, or at least uninterested in, everything else but our immediate need: air, at first. Just imagine the shock of breathing the first breath of air after having lived for nine months in water (not to mention the spanking doctor!!).

Then, having found that there is plenty of air, we immediately scream for our next most immediate necessity: food. Having received enough of what we want, we rest, till the next urge gets us screaming again. It is clear that we are driven, at least at first, by our physiological needs.

But, what about our mind? How does the newborn perceive his and her new existence, the new reality? On one side, the five senses of touch, sight, sound, smell and taste form what seems like a single sensory system designed to perceive physical reality and define a person's experience. On the other side, there are other types of perception, those involved with the mind and the heart: intuitions, thoughts, emotions, and other sensations. They are less visible and measurable, but are undoubtedly real and often influence our perception of reality.

Rational thoughts, bright ideas, hunches and insights have definitely assisted the human race in its evolutionary path. And, as we will see further on, it is in this less tangible world that we find the roots of our beliefs, our visions and our values.

Technically speaking, we could say that, from the moment we are born, (1) we feel new sensations, (2) absorb new information, (3) interpret new experiences, (4) develop new ideas, (5) make new choices, (6) envision new concepts. The process is somewhat complicated by the fact that there is a constant coming and going between sensual (I mean the five senses) perceptions and the mental interpretations of those sensations.

Buddhism teaches of rising ("chakra") centers of perception, from the molecular level, to the material, the animal (instinctive), the emotional (heart), the intellectual (mind), the soul, and finally the total perception of the Self.

Unfortunately, some experiences and the perceptions that they leave behind seem to have merely a negative or destructive side. But in the end, they teach us valuable lessons. Any child learns very quickly that trying to touch the dancing flames of an open fire has very unpleasant results, and if we ever did spit against the wind, we do not need to repeat the experience to remember it for life.

Sometimes our perception of reality seems to introduce us to a cold, unforgiving world full of dangers and pain. If our experiences are too painful, we may develop a pessimistic outlook. We may think: "I'll never succeed; I'll always have these pains." Sometimes, we empower negative memories that haunt us for years. Some psychologists think that, as long as we believe that we have been hurt, that we are inferior or treated unfairly, or that we have lost something or someone that can never be replaced, we will continue to feel that loss and pain.

To avoid pessimism and depression, we need to learn to perceive correctly and interpret our insights with a positive outlook, we need to interpret the data we receive in a constructive way. We need to avoid real germs as well as mental viruses. We need to filter our experiences to make sure that, whatever we are allowing to enter our hearts and minds will enrich us, and that the experiences we had and the ones we still pursue will add positive values to our lives and to the lives of our significant others.

Pain is a positive educational tool built in our binary matrix. We could over-simplify by saying that human beings are moved by two basic desires: we seek pleasure and we try to avoid pain. Our bodies use pain to let us know that something is going wrong, that we are out of sync, that there is something that is not part of our normal working condition, something that is or that will bring us harm. Similarly, our mind and our conscience (for those who still have one in working condition, and that exclude some top Enron executives) try to let us know when something is not working right.

The important point is: binary thought. *Human beings perceive and form their thoughts primarily using a binary system.* The binary system consists of the dual concept "one-many," which derives from the original "Self-others," and that expresses itself further in the dual (but inter-connected) worlds of our internal and external realities.

I bet Bill Gates would love this binary operating system. But, believe me, I did not make it up just to support the ideas he vaguely formulated in his latest book, *Business @ the Speed of Thought.* Even though, I must admit he's got some good intuitions concerning what he calls the "nervous digital network."

But, binary thought should not be confused with some mystical yin-yang theory. It must be viewed only as the lowest common denominator of human perception, the in-born concepts and *forma-mentis* (from Latin: form-of-the-mind) that constitute the essence of humans everywhere.

Just like the two inborn elements of "one" and "many" in abstract algebra cannot be described but only understood intuitively (like time and space), so binary thought is just one way (certainly not the only one, but I believe the most efficient and effective way at this particular time) to understand the way men and women perceive, think, value and behave.

WHAT TRUTH?

A binary truth

"Tonight we eat microwave food. I have no time to make dinner. The bus was late, and I'm tired as hell." Maggie O'Reilly sat in front of the television with her three sons, Mark, 17, Michael, 14, and Rob, 12. Her husband had gone out one fine, Sunday morning last spring to get a wedding cake for her cousin in nearby Londonderry. But he never came back. Patrick died from a sniper's bullet and was buried in St. John's Catholic Cemetery the following Tuesday.

It was a small flat. Too small for her and her three kids. There wasn't enough money, but she insisted that the kids go to school for as long as possible. The TV showed the pictures of seven British soldiers killed in an ambush in Northern Ireland, the reprisal for three IRA men killed earlier. "Will my children be next?" The thought of not knowing, living with that fearful doubt, made the pain all the more unbearable.

Maggie dropped the remote and began crying . . . again. How many have died for the sake of religion! How many more will? And, for what?

Speaking of perception, a short footnote is due on a special kind of perception: religious perception, religious experience, and the presumed purpose of religion.

It is hard to understand the real purpose of religion and the reason for man's search for spiritual enlightenment. Many people believe the purpose of religion is the search for truth. This has caused endless bickering among those who assume to know "the" truth, and its "right" interpretation. But truth is hard to find and even harder to define.

Even though the meaning of the word *truth* seems to be obvious, it is actually extremely difficult to formulate an acceptable definition of the term. The very notion of truth is based more on an intuitive insight than on a scientific thought construction, even though the search for truth seems to be claimed exclusively by those avenues of investigation that call themselves, precisely, "scientific."

Philosophers, epistemologists, theologians and other scholars of every persuasion have so far been unable to offer a clear, unambiguous assessment of the various existing definitions of the concept of "truth", and they have not been able to reconcile the numerous interpretations of it. Philosophical speculations have actually been the source of additional misconceptions and contradictions regarding this term.

Many of those who, throughout the centuries, have attempted

70

to define what truth really is, have done so by starting not so much from objective and measurable data (as would be characteristic of the scientific method), but rather from fideistic assumptions. The history of human thought has thus been marked by a confrontation between faith and science and between paradigms belonging to the past and the future. But it doesn't need to be so. Before going any further, let me assure the reader that I maintain excellent relations with Catholic representatives. I even presented the Italian version of this book to His Holiness Pope John Paul II.

Everyone remembers the confrontation between Galileo Galilei and the Catholic Church in the first half of the 17th Century. Galileo was summoned by the Inquisition to explain his convictions (i.e., that the Earth, considered until then as the center of the universe, being the planet chosen by God to be the home of his favorite creature, human beings, was actually revolving around the sun and not the opposite), and he was subsequently forced to formally recant his findings. In spite of this, the Inquisition ordered his writings to be burned in 1633, and he had to spend the last eight years of his life in house arrest. At that time, like many other times before and after, scientific evidence was met by the so-called moral force of faith, or rather by the human fears of those who were unable to administer that faith except by terrorist means.

When a human being is convinced that he or she knows and possesses the only unique and unquestionable Truth, this conviction can be so deep that, in a great many cases, people have been willing to sacrifice even their very lives in order to defend their ideals (this is particularly true in the case of religious beliefs). In fact, the number of early widows in Ireland could easily be topped by those in the Middle East, in India, in Pakistan, in Afghanistan, etc.

Thus, truth does not only require us to believe in it, it also expects us to lift its banner with pride, even when this means a real sacrifice.

Unfortunately, not all believers are willing to sacrifice

themselves. Many more people have been willing to sacrifice other people's lives (see recent examples in the Talibans' Afghanistan, Saddam's Iraq, Milosevich's Serbia, Rwanda, Somalia, and so on) instead of their own and often with greater enthusiasm, efficiency and exuberance.

It seems, however, that even the most meticulous investigations, be they of a spiritual, philosophical or scientific type, are unable to uncover the whole (!#@!*x!) Truth.

What we can actually achieve, on the other hand, are so many small and partial truths (lower case!). As for the One, Big Truth about the meaning of life and the world, the origin and purpose of the universe and the existence of God, I think we should be satisfied when and if we can even approach it as that great example of wonderful British theatrical humor, *Monty Python and the Holy Grail,* clearly shows (I confess, I am a great fan of most of the Monty Python movies).

On the positive side, we must admit that man's trust in the existence of one big Truth is also expressed by his sharing and passing on all the little truths he or she, as an individual, can make his own. Thus, the sharing of beneficial information, insights and innovations with the greater community allows progress and growth.

The search for big and small truths has always had great importance in all societies and in all ages. Almost all cultures and societies of the past and present have had and continue to have a particular respect and admiration for those who have the courage to risk their lives in the search for truth and thus manage to catch a glimpse of it, becoming its messengers, illuminating humankind in the light of their discovery.

We all love big and small truths, not just wisdom revealed by prophets and saints or scientific research into the cause of cancer or the workings of germs and viruses, but also more mundane truth. Smaller truths, like the truth about polluted waters (here the success of the movie *Erin Brokovich*), cigarettes' relationship to lung cancer, as well as not-yet-released little truths about UFOs,

Nixon's tapes, and Clinton's lady-friends; well, it can be a long, boring and unpleasant list.

In conclusion, we notice a parallel track: on one side, men and women seek truthful information regarding the external world in which we live; on the other side, there is a quest for deep answers to more personal questions dealing with our inner lives.

Being consistent with the binary categories described before, it would follow that the internal desire for happiness and fulfillment leads man to search for information dealing with the inner aspects of our lives, and that is the realm of religion, philosophy, and spirituality, while the desire for strictly physiological well-being, pleasure, comfort, and more mundane joys often find its answers within the realm of scientific investigation. *A binary type of truth,* if you like: one internal type of information is addressed to the inner self, the other is external, addressed to the external world. Both types are often overlapping, complementary if you want, but also quite distinct and sometimes conflicting.

RELATIONS

The binary and inter-relational nature of truth

Immanuel Kant (1724-1804), the great German philosopher, in the conclusion of his pace-setting work: *The Critique of Practical Reason* (1788) skillfully describes the binary nature of human perception.

Two things fill the mind with ever new and increasing admiration and awe, the oftener and the more steadily we reflect on them: the starry heavens above and the moral law within. I have not to search for them and conjecture them as though they were veiled in darkness or were in the transcendent region beyond my horizon; I see them before me and connect them directly with the consciousness of my existence.

The former begins from the place I occupy in the external world of sense, and enlarges my connection therein to an unbounded extent with worlds upon worlds and systems of systems, and moreover into limitless times of their periodic motion, its beginning and continuance.

The second begins from my invisible self, my personality, and exhibits me in a world which has true infinity, but which is traceable only by the understanding, and with which I discern that I am not in a merely contingent but in a universal and necessary connection, as I am also thereby with all those visible worlds.

The former view of a countless multitude of worlds annihilates as it were my importance as an animal creature, which after it has been for a short time provided with vital power, one knows not how, must again give back the matter of which it was formed to the planet it inhabits (a mere speck in the universe).

The second, on the contrary, infinitely elevates my worth as an intelligence by my personality, in which the moral law reveals to me a life independent of animality and even of the whole sensible world, at least so far as may be inferred from the destination assigned to my existence by this law, a destination not restricted to conditions and limits of this life, but reaching into the infinite.

What can I add to such delicate and yet profound sentences? What I write is but a sloppy summary of what has been told before.

Kant's comprehensive studies on the theory of knowledge, ethics, and aesthetics brought to new heights the trends of Rationalism (stressing reason, as begun by the French philosopher René Descartes) and Empiricism (stressing experience, led by the British Francis Bacon), pioneering a modern form of Idealism.

"The starry heaven above" is the infinite number of things out there. "The moral law within" is what I call the Self. The former is perceived by our senses as an external world, while the second begins with our invisible self, our self-awareness and the understanding of an inner world, equally limitless and full of wonders. What is important is that, as in the case of other binary concepts—such as "one and many", "inside and outside", "before and after", "good and bad", and "pleasure and pain"—the most effective way of describing the way humans judge or evaluate a thing or a situation is by using BI-POLAR scales. This seems to confirm the relational nature of our forma-mentis, our binary pattern of thought.

So, our perception of reality can be expressed also as a bipolar relationship: I—myself and I—the world. The first one relates to the relationship we have with our own selves (self-identity), our awareness of our singular entity (the one). The other relationship, between us and the world (others), involves the concept of many. The first is internal, the second more external.

Our perceptions can be similarly divided between those relative to our inner self: our intuitions, feelings, thoughts and ideas, and those relative to our external self: touch, smell, sight, hearing and taste.

Somehow, our inner sensations have more to do with our self-identity and with our consciousness of the self as one entity, while our external senses deal primarily with the world out there and the innate concept of plurality. I am not suggesting a dogma but rather observing the way the human mind seems to perceive and understand itself and the reality that surrounds it. I do not want in any shape or form to endorse Oriental philosophies or any form of dualism; rather, I am trying to observe human perception from a different (more digital) perspective.

In conclusion, we could say that, based on the binary world of one-many, we can observe another binary system: that which is internal, within the mind, and that which is "out there", distinct and seemingly independent from our own existence. Thus, from one-many we derive another basic binary construct: in-out. From these two constructs, we create a system of relations: a relational, binary matrix.

SYMMETRY AND RELATIONALITY

From one-many to in-out

Having developed a binary system, a relational system based on the two elementary concepts of Me-World, One-Many, we start to notice symmetry.

As infants, we find symmetry in the facial features of mom, nurse, and that darn doctor that spanked us as soon as we got out of mom's watery womb. Later, we notice more symmetry, from other aspects of the human body (at least its exterior), to the exterior form of most animals and plants.

Have you ever noticed how symmetry permeates almost all of nature? We are often attracted to beautiful symmetrical faces (and proportional bodies), while we dislike uneven ones. But why symmetry seems to manifest itself always between right and left sides and not between upper and lower parts, I do not know.

This external (right-left) symmetry further influences our perception of reality, reinforcing the binary structure of the baby's mind. Now we can understand how this binary system has influenced many ancient civilizations.

Even today, many cultures interpret this symmetry and the relational bi-polarism of the human mind as a universal "pattern," concluding that reality is made of bi-polar or complementary elements. Not me. I am *not* supporting one or another view of reality. I just propose *a new way of organizing* our perception of ourselves and what surrounds us.

Many of the world's religions and philosophies, from ancient times to the present, have noticed symmetry in nature and a relationship of complementarity among living beings. As a result, they have derived some sort of transcendent "laws" that should be at work in the whole cosmos.

So, is symmetry real or just perceived? I do not know. But it is a fact that most religions uphold a bipolar, complementary view of nature (even though Ying and Yang can be interpreted in different ways, and while the Judeo-Christian-Islamic tradition has not extrapolated much out of the man/woman duality).

For them, and many other religions as well, all existence, all living beings great and small, are linked in a web of interdependence and complex relationships. Every relationship has a certain "duality" and a certain order. There is dynamic, mutual movement, and exchange between male and female, heaven and earth, mind and matter, light and dark, being and non-being, substance and void, this and that, myself and others, and one and many.

This movement within and between beings in synergistic relationships is the source of life and creative power. We could say that from the binary system of one-many evolves the concept of in-out, like a circle and its center or a sphere and its center.

From this binary matrix we start to observe a sort of symmetry, and, when the matrix gets applied to motion, we notice symmetry in motion, like the sound of our breathing in and out, the flow of blood going in and out of our heart, the ocean waves washing in and out of the beach.

At this point, we must remember that it is *only* with the ability to *freely* move and freely associate that life itself is maintained and evolves. Thus, freedom is one of the essential ingredients for life itself. In Hindu beliefs, this motion is often seen in the regular cycles of nature, the changing seasons. The cosmic union of god and goddess and male and female principles sometimes mythically represent this life and freedom principle.

I do not subscribe to the universality of human perception, but I rather believe that we, as human beings, do perceive reality according to some categories that are inscribed in our genetic makeup. Of course, for all practical purposes, we may as well assume some sort of transcendent law, but I do not exclude the possibility, albeit further remote, that a radical change in the human psyche and/or a sudden jump in the "evolution" of mankind, like mutations introduced by the manipulation of human DNA, may bring a change in the way our minds perceive reality.

Since the process of perception can be reduced to a bi-polar, binary matrix, we can now apply this newfound knowledge to our quest for value and the meaning of value (evaluation, the way we make choices, we judge others, ourselves and the world, and the concept of purpose), as well as to other elements in the fields of economics and social studies.

END NOTES

Abstract Algebra: Al-Jabar and the Arab World

The binary construct of "one-many" happens to be one of algebra's most fundamental concepts, and algebra brings us to the Arab world. While Europe was experiencing the so-called "Dark Ages", roughly from 600 A.D. to 1200 A.D., the torch of ancient Greek learning was passed on to that strong invading force that helped bring down the Eastern Roman Empire: Islam.

In the 7th Century after the birth of Jesus of Nazareth, the Arabs, inspired by their Great Prophet, Mohammed (PBUH, as the brothers and sisters say) burst out of the Arabian Peninsula and laid the foundations of an Islamic empire that eventually rivaled that of ancient Rome. To the ancient Arabs, knowledge (and science) was a precious treasure (and, hence, one of the reasons for the early success of this great civilization).

The Q'uran, the sacred book of Islam (the word Islam means "surrender," surrender to the will of Allah, the sole God, Creator, Sustainer and Restorer of the world), particularly praised medicine as an art close to God. Astronomy and astrology were believed to be ways of glimpsing into what Allah intended to manifest to His people.

It was also contact with Roman practical sciences, Greek philosophy and Hindu mathematics, as well as the requirements of astronomy that stimulated the study of numbers and of geometry. The writings of the ancient Romans and Hellenes were, therefore, eagerly sought and translated; thus, much of the sciences of antiquity passed into Islamic culture. By the end of the 9th century, medicine, astronomy, astrology, and mathematics, together with the great philosophical works of Plato and Aristotle, were assimilated into Islamic culture and tradition. But, the Arabs did not stop with assimilation. They criticized and they innovated.

Islamic astronomy and astrology were aided by the construction of great astronomical observatories that provided accurate observations against which the Ptolemaic predictions could be checked. Numbers fascinated Islamic thinkers, and this fascination served as the motivation for the study of algebra (from the Arabic "al-jabar") and the study of algebraic functions.

Thought and Relations. From elementary algebra evolved the abstract algebra used today and the idea of an algebraic structure. Elementary algebra was originally concerned with a set of elements: numbers. In addition to numbers, there were two basic operations: addition and multiplication (subtraction and division being the inverse of these). Algebra, like mathematics, is organized according to a set of primary rules that are often referred to as an axiomatic structure. The axiomatic structure describes the rules as well as the assumptions made in elementary algebra and arithmetic.

Sometimes, though, not all elements follow these rules. Abstract algebra is concerned with the formulation and properties of this type. These systems are sets of elements with general operations and with a number of specific axioms. Just as some geometries can be based on axioms other than those of Euclid (you may have heard of 4, 5 dimensional spaces), abstract algebra can be based on axioms that differ from those of elementary algebra.

Now, we come to the good part. Two of the most basic elements that abstract algebra deals with are the two fundamental concepts of "ONE" and "MANY" and the theory of groups. One and many are considered inborn concepts that cannot be derived or described from other representations. A branch of algebra that began to take shape in the early days of the 19th century, the theory of groups was first studied by Abel and Galois and later by Lie, Klein and by the English mathematician (mainly known as a religious philosopher), Alfred North Whitehead.

Another important element in abstract algebra is the duality principle, where, for any category, 1, interchanging the domains and codomains of the morphisms of 1 can form a new category, 0.

The duality principle has very wide ramifications because this apparently trivial operation leads to highly significant results when specific categories are used. In the general setting, it enables any concept in the language of categories to be dualized. Also, group theory brings us back to the binary concept of one and many. Groups, in mathematics, are systems of elements that satisfy certain rules. The elements may be operations or the symmetries of a geometrical figure. Not until the late 18th and 19th centuries, however, were groups recognized as mathematical systems. The French mathematician, Joseph-Louis Lagrange, was one of the first to consider them, followed by other French mathematicians, like Augustin-Louis Cauchy and Évariste Galois. The concept of groups (one and many are the two inborn and irreducible concepts needed to define a "group") is now recognized as one of the most essential in all of mathematics and in many of its applications.

Decision problems

Returning to a binary way of defining categories, it is interesting to note that, in the scientific investigation into decision-making problems, for a class of questions in mathematics and formal logic, when the answer is indeed one or the other, one or zero: a binary system. (For example, the problem of finding, after choosing any question of the class, an algorithm or repetitive procedure that will yield a definite answer, "yes" or "no" to that question, that, too, is binary). The method consists of performing successively a finite number of steps determined by pre-assigned rules. In particular, this technique is used for such procedures as finding whether, in a particular logistic system, logical calculus, or formal mathematical system, some given "well-formed formula" (generated in accordance with established formation rules) is or is not provable as a theorem of the system.

Binary and relational information

Within the realm of the philosophical sciences, epistemology deals with the issue of knowing *how we know what we know* and *how truth is perceived and understood.* Regarding the notion of truth itself, epistemology tries to answer the following question: Under what exact circumstances are we justified in calling something true or false? In philosophy, this is called the isle of the *criteria of truth*, which is precisely the object of epistemology.

Philosophically speaking, the systematic search for truth has its foundation in ancient Greece, with Socrates (469-399 B.C.), Plato (427-347 B.C.), and, particularly, with Aristotle's (384-322 B.C.) *Metaphysics* and his *De Interpretatione*.

Aristotle focused on the truth of a sentence; he considered truth to be *a possible quality of propositions.* The meaningful application of this quality of "truthfulness" is limited to *apophantic* (affirmative or negative) propositions. In this way, a statement can have only two alternatives: "true" or "false". This, argued Aristotle, seems to apply not only to propositions, but also to parts of what is endowed with meaning, since even parts of a sentence can have meaning.

For Aristotle, meaningfulness is, therefore, a necessary prerequisite for the true/false alternative to apply at all. A proposition can thus only be true or false if it is endowed with meaning; in the contrary case, it can be neither true nor false. The whole question appears to be rather complex, but, if we switch from the domain of epistemology to that of *ontology* (the "study of being," the study of the nature of things, and the nature of reality), we soon realize that only that which can be expressed and experienced or understood is real, or exists, while that which cannot be expressed (because it has no meaning) cannot exist. The categories of true and false can, therefore, also be applied to the criteria of the existence of reality.

The ontological dimension of the notion of truth is more obvious with Plato, for whom the opposition is not only between true and false, but also between truth and appearance, i.e., between that which "is" in an absolute way and to an absolute degree and that which only has an inferior and derivative type of existence. In this case, the notion of truth is applied to the relationship between the higher being and existing beings or between God as the ultimate truth and mankind and the world as a mere appearance. We should add that for Plato, there was no God, as we understand it today, but rather lower case gods that could be understood only in the realm of ideas.

Plato described this relationship in the so-called "Myth of the Cave." Imagine a gigantic cave. You are in the cave, trying to see in the dim light, trying to distinguish shapes and forms. You cannot see the outside of the cave, but some of the light filters through, and, on a great stone wall, you can see some shadows moving on it. You do not see the real figures, just their shadows. From that, you try to figure out what those images represent. From the shapes, forms and movements of the shadows, you try to understand the true nature of the things moving outside the cave in the sunlight.

For Plato, the real world lies beyond the senses, outside the cave. What we perceive and understand is but a distorted and partial shade of a transcendent world. I think Plato would have loved the movie, *Matrix*. To be fair to Plato, we should add that Christianity added the Divine Dimension. The Greek philosopher simply acknowledged ignorance of the world beyond.

With the advent of Christianity, the identification of truth with God Himself finds its expression in the words of the Gospel of John: "*I am the Way, the Truth and the Life.*" On the basis of the Trinitarian dogma, this also amounts to an identification of God with the Word of God. It follows that, in an ontological sense, even material objects are "true," since every element of Creation is seen as being present in the archetypal idea within the mind of God that has been the model for His creation. In scholasticism, the word "true" is actually categorized among the *transcendentals*, i.e., the propositions that qualify the nature of being, a notion that extends to all existing beings.

This ontological understanding of the word will be overshadowed and replaced by a logical understanding, beginning with the work of Thomas Aquinas, in the fifth century, and going on until Hobbes, Spinoza and Locke. This road eventually leads to Kantian criticism.

With Immanuel Kant's insights into the *limits and possibilities of reason,* it became possible to attribute a predicate to a subject (a judgment = the only criteria of verifiability of reality). Kant dealt with ontology only to the extent that it relates to the phenomenal world (not counting the realm of faith), and his work precisely forms the philosophical threshold to the age of epistemology, the modern and contemporary age that often dismisses ontological questions as irrelevant or unsolvable. Hegel resurrected and systematized the *ontological momentum*, which identified truth with the Idea, and thus considered truth as what is *"true in itself."*

Even one seeming opponent of the "relational" system, John Locke, considered by many to be one of the most prominent practical philosophers of 17th century England, somehow supports the complementary nature of the human "forma-mentis." Locke believed that almost all of our knowledge is derived from sense perceptions and introspection. In his principal work, the *Essay Concerning Human Understanding*, Locke tried to dispose of the theory of innate ideas. For Locke, knowledge consisted of the understanding of the connection between agreement and disagreement among our ideas, "identity and diversity."

Similarly to Locke, I do believe that, in normal circumstances, reality is perceived through two modes: 1. Our five physical senses, and 2. The emotions and/or thoughts that are induced by experiences. Unfortunately, our experiences do not always reflect reality. Sometimes, we ascribe to our experiences deeper and/or different meanings, so that appearances are often taken as signs or even symbols referring to an underlying reality.

Sometimes, however, appearances are incompatible with facts, like a mirror, or a mirage, an optical illusion, like an oar in water that looks broken but feels straight to the touch. It must be determined, if one is to have a coherent picture of reality, which appearances are illusory and may lead to error regarding the real. Because the status of appearance is equivocal, one is forced to distinguish between those appearances and perceptions that correspond with reality and those that are more or less illusory.

The distinction between "real" and "not quite real" will depend on a conception of reality that can serve as a criterion for judging appearances. Here is the key: whatever is conformable to one's conception of the real will be given value; whatever is opposed to it will be denied value. Every concept can be subjected to a similar dissociation of appearance and reality.

Real freedom, real democracy, real justice and real happiness can be opposed to apparent freedom or democracy, false justice or a make-believe happiness. The former, being in conformity with the criteria of what freedom, justice, democracy, and happiness really are, will keep the value normally attached to these notions. By means of this technique of dissociating concepts, some philosophers did try to direct men's actions toward what they held to be true values, rejecting those values that they considered only apparent. Every ontology, or theory about the nature of being, makes use of this philosophical process that gives value to certain aspects of reality and denies it to others according to dissociations that it justifies by developing a particular conception of reality.

Buddhist teachings distinguish between different types of perception. Perception of reality grows as people move from different types of experience—from the material, to the animal, the sensual, the emotional, the mental, the experience of the soul, and ending with the religious experience. Each type of experience and perception opens the gate to a different world, a different reality. But this system creates too many categories and, frankly, too much confusion.

A binary system is more simple and clear.

In the second half of the 18th century, David Hume noted that human beings have the tendency to attribute a cause and effect relationship to events that are apparently interrelated. Whenever two events repeatedly coincide (even if this is purely by chance or unintentional), people learn to expect the second event to happen as soon as the first one occurs, or the opposite. Let us take the example of two clocks that are perfectly synchronized, so that if the first one rings, the second one does likewise. The unscientific observer will tend to imagine that there is some kind of a relationship between the two clocks, while, in reality, there is only a parallel and simultaneous action.

Some time after Hume challenged the relational nature of cause and effect, Jevons, Menger and Walras, with the theory of marginalism, introduced, in economics, one of the most interesting cause and effect relationships ever proposed in the new discipline.

Between 1871 and 1874, Jevons (England), Menger (Germany), and Walras (Switzerland) published practically at the same time, but independently from one another, three different treatises on economics and, more specifically, on the theory of prices. Their works ended up having a considerable influence in their field, and their impact can still be felt today. With their particular theories on the determination of relative prices, the marginalists (as they are called) tried to prove that the prime cause of the determination of value does not lie in a mechanism that starts with the production costs and ends with the final price of a commodity, but that, instead, there is a reverse mechanism beginning with the sales price and leading back to the production process.

Their idea was that *the means of production do not determine the price, but that the means are determined by the price customers are willing to pay for a commodity*.

We can say that a certain amount of skepticism must have stimulated in some way the development of philosophical thought, as well as that of scientific research. A certain level of caution is always to be recommended (in the case of economics, in particular, where being gullible is definitely not a virtue), but being skeptical should in no way lead one to eliminate *a priori* all avenues that could lead to an unexpected result or be so cautious as to resort only to obsolete models and stereotypes and, thus, end up in senility (even though senility is one of the most frequent characteristics of economists).

In the search for truth, pragmatism can sometimes be necessary (I am not implying, though, that this should lead us to David Hume's excessive skepticism or Herbert Spencer's agnosticism). Pragmatism may especially be advisable in cases where the issue is to defend (or disseminate) the idea underlying those notions that are most essential to the survival of civilization, a significant and vital example being the notions of *democracy* and *liberty* (as we will see in the next chapter).

A functional definition

I would like to propose an applied or functional definition of the concept of truth. It is based on what I call: ***The principle of correlativity of human perception.*** According to this principle, truth in itself cannot be defined; I would even dare to add that truth, as an entity in itself, does not exist. ***Human beings perceive reality only in a relational matrix. We perceive and define things (including our own self) only as relationships to other things or to other sentient beings.***

Human beings perceive the reality of the senses, and even their own selves, in an *inter-relational* manner. For this reason, we can infer that truth itself is perceived in an inter-relational way. In other words, truth exists only in terms of a relationship between two elements (truth as correspondence).

A proposition is true if facts are as it *says* they are. If facts are not as the proposition states they are, the proposition is false.

Generally speaking, the two elements constituting the bi-polar relationship that forms the basis for the notion of truth are *words/actions* or *concepts/facts*, i.e., a symbolism through the medium of the word and the actual data to which it refers. In that sense, we could conclude that there are only *true propositions*, i.e., a dialectical relationship between two seemingly antithetical elements, namely an abstract concept, an idea, an expression, a symbol, and the concrete reality as it is thus described.

What makes a proposition (and the underlying belief) true or false is the presence or absence of a relationship of *correspondence* between the proposition and facts, regardless of any experience one may have of them. Hence, a true proposition is one in which the words used to describe a concept are actually, clearly, a reflection of an *objective* reality. What I mean by objective reality is a reality that can be observed in the same way and simultaneously by several observers, regardless of the time and perspective. Let us summarize the above in a diagram:

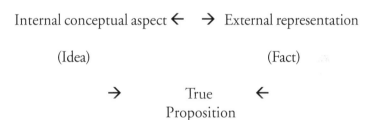

Internal conceptual aspect ← → External representation

(Idea)   (Fact)

→   True   ←
Proposition

This leads us straight into the field of the philosophy of language, which is not of interest here and will only be touched upon briefly. In the philosophy of language, the notion of truth as a correspondence is expressed in a particularly accurate and precise way in the following thesis: the proposition "A is B" can be considered true if and only if A **is** B. From this, we can then conclude that *true* and *false* are secondary predicates, in the sense that they refer to the *mention* of a proposition or to its *name*. It is, therefore, necessary to distinguish between objective language (whenever a particular proposition is being used in order to speak of something else) and *metalanguage* (i.e., when the issue that is being discussed is the proposition itself).

By introducing the above distinction, which is unknown in the realm of natural languages, one can avoid being trapped by the well-known "paradox of the liar" (if I say, "I am lying," what I am stating is true only if it is not true). Since ancient times, this paradox has in fact been presented as the typical antinomy pertaining to the notion of truth and used as a popular demonstration of the belief that ultimately truth cannot be known, while, to the attentive listener, the pseudo-paradox is only a play of words.

According to the new binary matrix, the concept of a **relational truth** can be considered to be one of the inborn notions of the human mind. And, even though, in the history of philosophy, truth as a relationship of correspondence is only one of the key notions of truth, its relational nature remains constant. I am certain that, in the future, it will certainly be possible to find more accurate and comprehensive definitions of what "truth" is supposed to mean, but these definitions will inevitably have to take into consideration the relational nature of the human frame of mind; hence, these definitions will have to present themselves in a bipolar, relational mode.

I hope that these few lines and the "relational" perspective I have just introduced can stimulate the thought of those, wherever they stand, who are trying to deal with unanswered questions, existential doubts, and difficulties in grasping the meaning of reality. Well, maybe they just got even more confused—sorry!

Some say the Truth will set you free. Some say it will also make you happy, but that's more debatable. On the one hand, it is very useful to know how things work and where we can find those things that we believe are going to make us happy.

Some people say that the purpose of religion is to find love or to experience love. Love is certainly the most important value for the great majority of human beings today, as it has been for thousands of years, and it is also true that one of the most fundamental needs and desires of human beings the world over is the desire to receive and share love. On the other hand, it is also true that no culture or society has been able to maintain its existence based solely on this wonderful emotion. Clearly, man does not live on bread alone, but it is equally true that man cannot live without bread. So, religion, in the narrower sense of the word, cannot fulfill all human needs and desires, just like material possessions (and economies) are not sufficient to completely fulfill man's quest for happiness.

CHAPTER III

NECESSITIES

What's important?

During a television interview years ago, Robert De Niro was asked what he thought the reason was for his success. "Why do people go to the movies?" replied De Niro. Then he continued, "Because movies give people what they need."

If you like action movies, you probably saw *Three Kings* with George Clooney. In the middle of the Iraqi desert, facing a difficult choice, the Captain (Clooney) asks: "What's the most important thing?"

"Respect," answers one soldier.

"Wrong answer. What's the most important thing?" repeats the Captain.

"Love," says another soldier.

"Disneyland," says George Clooney with a grin. Then he gives "THE" answer: "Necessities. Whatever is most needed at the time."

And, that's the final answer. Of course, later in the movie,

those same necessities changed, but that's the nature of things . . .
or is it? Even though there are differences of meaning between
needs, wants and desires, throughout this book I have used the
terms without making real distinctions (even though I recognize
their differences) and, quite often, I have used them
interchangeably.

But, I need to make a small distinction here between two
types of drives: those that are inborn in our nature (determined
by our physiology, and our genes) and those drives (needs, desires,
wants, fears, etc.) that are typical of a specific individual,
determined by one's particular experiences, environment, culture,
values, and choices.

The first drives are what I call our Basic Drives, those
implanted in the DNA of our every cell by Mother Nature, like
hunger, thirst, the need for oxygen, and that most troublesome
of all human drives: sex. Ouch!!! That is the tender spot of our
frail human matrix.

"Sex" and its nobler but equally troublesome partner, "Love",
have been hidden in our hormones, estrogen, testosterone and
who knows what else, since before birth. By the time puberty
kicks in, Nature's chemical warfare flares up, the time-released
emotional fireworks lighten the horizon and often even our
rational mind and most basic instincts fall prey to the consuming
passions. Occasionally, some courageous soul tries to fight Mother
Nature, maybe successfully for a short while, but we can all find
greater freedom when we acknowledge that we are enslaved, to a
certain extent, by our genetic make-up. And, even if we could try
to live without sex or love of any kind, we certainly cannot live
without air, food or water. So, as Saint Francis said, "Lord, give
me Patience with the things I cannot change, Strength with those
I can change, and the Wisdom to know the difference."

The things we can change, and often do change, are what I
call *Acquired Drives*. These are our needs, desires, and values
that were learned in school or at home, encouraged by teachers
and advertisers, and often frustrated by society (such as Mary's
absolute need for a new dress, Joanne's recurrent desire for a diet

that will reduce her "spare tire," Joe's compulsive gambling, and Carl's impulsive twitch in the right foot to press down the pedal every time some punk kid on a Honda comes too close to his low-riding Ford Mustang).

Changing our value system can often modify all these and other acquired drives. But knowledge, or even wisdom alone, is not sufficient to make changes in our acquired drives. Unless you make the decision yourself, other forces come to assert their power against you. From childhood on, each individual makes a decision, conscious or unconscious, sometimes in the blink of an eye, to accept or reject the values implied in the acquired drives, and so each person can make a choice to keep or change his or her drives (desires, wants, perceived needs, fears, and values).

Somewhere between basic and acquired drives are other needs, psychological needs, such as the need for affection and security, the need to communicate and interact with others, and other needs as well; these will be dealt with in the chapter on cultural values and behavior.

BASIC AND ACQUIRED NEEDS

Things we can and cannot do without

In our so-called developed culture, technology has advanced to the point where obtaining the basic needs of food, clothing and shelter are no longer impossible problems. Our genetic heritage determines those essential needs—like food, water and air—but we also need some form of clothing and shelter, in a manner almost identical to that of our hunting and gathering Stone Age ancestors.

Basic Drives, such as hunger, thirst, sex, and also security, community, etc., are innate, inherited. The other drives are acquired, encouraged by family and society, sometimes frustrated by tradition or culture. Some needs may be real; others can be perceived. Others are a mixture of both, like the need to affiliate with others, to achieve, to be acknowledged, to be successful, etc. But, when speaking of success, one word of caution is necessary.

In the U.S.A., our inborn desire to achieve and be successful can be manipulated and distorted, and the culture of "success at all costs" can be carried too far. The inevitable shortcomings derived from the excessive value placed on being "first" (not everyone can arrive first, rather the opposite; just about everyone arrives after) are many and not very constructive, like debilitating feelings of frustration, jealousy, bitterness, hurt, envy, stress, anger, and sometimes aggression.

It is ok to encourage a child's desire to achieve and be recognized and appreciated, but it is equally important to do so in a positive way. It is imperative to break the destructive conditioning—that Darwinian "eat or be eaten" mind-set that ignorant and insensitive media manipulators try to load on our backs. If you are the proud father of a teenage daughter, you know that uncontrollable urge she has to shop 'til she drops once you get to the local Mall. Thinking about that and other excessive Christmas shopping, we notice that the inevitable limits on the amount of objects that one can possess, and the constant propaganda of the advertising media, culture and peer pressure, create the premises for the inevitable and continuous frustration and dissatisfaction, even among the wealthiest of individuals.

When faced with frustration and stress, we should break the conditioning that makes us act the way others think we should act and desire what others think we should have. The culture of "Number One" is often carried too far, not just in the U.S. and in western nations, but also in Asia and elsewhere. The inevitable results are that many people (women in particular) feel depressed, frustrated, bitter, envious, etc. Since needs and desires determine behavior, often feelings of stress, frustration, and anger lead to destructive (even self-destructive) and/or aggressive behavior, like Joe kicking the dog when returning home from a bad day at the office, or Mary watching soap operas all day in order to escape from having to do the laundry. Aggression and denial *seem* to alleviate or reduce frustration because they help people let go of pent up feelings or try to resolve them by proxy.

SCROOGE

Conflicting Needs

It was late at night, and Scrooge had already faced his ghosts. He was alone, hiding under the old blankets, in the scarcely lit and cold bedroom. The smell of decay had already permeated everything in the house, and now it was slowly infecting his soul. Scrooge hadn't made up his mind yet. He was still facing his conflicting needs and desires. His mind did not want to give up the cozy, wonderful sense of security that money was giving him, while his aching heart yearned for the warmth of human touch and companionship. Ebenezer Scrooge had a hard time reconciling seemingly conflicting needs and desires.

"Money is not just security," Scrooge told himself, "it is also the product of hard work, the clear and tangent proof of my hard days and nights of diligent and painful work." Outside the snow was still falling. The dark, the cold and the silence were hard to bear. "What's wrong with money? Nothing, nothing," he was talking aloud now. "So why do I feel so empty?"

Scrooge put his head in his hands. "Maybe because it is not enough." His tone was softer, now, sadder. He could not even recognize his own voice when he said: "It is not the money that is wrong, it is thinking only of my security that makes me lonely. I can't be happy caring only about me. It gets boring. I need to be with other people, think about other things, care about more than just me."

A very small tear, almost invisible, tried to go past his eyelashes. It did not go far, it dried up on the dry and cold skin. But the change had begun. A little warmth had begun in Scrooge's heart, and a tiny ghost of a smile had made its first appearance on his thin lips.

How many times do we find ourselves in a similar predicament? Like Scrooge, the main character of *A Christmas Carol* by Charles Dickens (I apologize for the small changes I made to the original story), one "side" of ourselves desires something while another side wants something else.

Have you ever been stuck in mile-long traffic jams? Sometimes, after inching along for 40 or 50 minutes on the highway, inhaling carbon dioxide from the truck in front of me and smoke from the bus next to me, my irrational desire is to scream and break something. But, then my rational conscience kicks in. What a pain! There is a fight going on between my rational self and my irrational emotions, but, then my more rational and "pain-in-the-rear" conscience kicks in and I turn on the radio, take a short deep breath, and let my hot blood cool off. Maybe it's one of those right side brains vs. left side brain things. In any case, it is important, particularly in business, as well as in our personal life, to set the right priorities.

To prioritize needs, goals and activities means to separate desires into different categories. We will look at the distinction between the desires of the rational mind and the often-irrational heart further on. Looking at needs and desires, we can distinguish between: 1. Basic desires—those inborn, can't-take-them-out-of-your-system desires, and 2. Acquired desires—those "I-can-really-also-live-without-it" ones. In Scrooge's case, his greed was, in part, the expression of his overpowering desire for financial security, a clearly "acquired" desire. On the other hand, his emotional need for warmth and love was certainly a more "basic" desire.

Those needs and desires that are closer to our truer and more profound nature can be classified as more "internal," while those desires and perceived needs that we pick up from our environment and experiences are often more "external." We can also call "internal desires" those that fulfill our internal needs (mental, emotional, spiritual), while "external desires" are those that generally fulfill our more material and physiological needs. Among a multitude of needs and desires, the desire for well-being, material comfort and financial security, for example, can be partly researched through the study of economics. Some internal needs and desires, like those dealing with the meaning and purpose of human life, have been dealt with by psychology, philosophy and, in their unique way, by the great world religions.

Scrooge had to deal with an existential question and a choice: the afterlife, his afterlife, and the possibility of changing his destiny from an early and lonely grave to a longer and fuller life. And even the master of Buddhist "detachment," the Dalai Lama (who I had the privilege to meet in many occasions), is attached to his people and to his land. He cannot just let go of his responsibility, his connection and his affections only because someone has come and kicked him out of his country. Of course, we are often enticed to return the harm we suffer with some form of retribution. But obstacles can also be seen as tests, challenges to be overcome. Temptations are not supposed to be fallen into. If we do not, we learn the lesson the easy way and go on. If you do fall for it, you learn the lesson the hard way and it takes longer to get to the next stage, not a bad system, after all.

So, let us take a brief and superficial look at these two essential areas of human endeavor: religion and economics. When we consider these two fields, we notice that some of their common ground is covered by the social sciences and by politics, but we also notice a close relationship between religion and economics and one important element that is common to both of them: value.

THE PURSUIT OF HAPPINESS

What everybody wants

In the great marble hall at the center of the Capitol Building in Washington, D.C., behind a bulletproof glass, there is an almost sacred document: the Constitution of the United States of America.

We all know the first part of the Constitution: "All men are created equal and are endowed with some unalienable rights among which are life, liberty and the pursuit of happiness."

No words have ever moved people and souls as deeply as these timeless words. No sentence can capture more clearly the essence of human values, needs and desires. After these simple yet universal words, it may be vain to try to expound on the quest for happiness, but let us analyze, alas superficially, like the rest of this book, the nature of this most important human quest.

Not to be repetitive, but this quest also has two facets. Like an old gold coin, the desire for happiness and pleasure has its reverse side in our fear of unpleasant things and our desire to avoid pain, misery and sorrow. Desire for pleasure and fear of pain seem to be encoded in our very DNA (and RNA, if we are to believe some of the latest theories.)

In speaking of happiness, we must speak also of suffering and pain, and, in dealing with unhappiness, one needs to understand its causes so as to be able to free one's self from it. Buddhism distinguishes between two types of cause-and-effect chains. One causal chain between suffering and its origins leads to an un-enlightened life, while the enlightened path pertains to truer and more compassionate causal links.

Before beginning toward the path of liberation, Buddhist teachings require that one acknowledge his or her suffering state (duhkha) and express a desire to escape the cycle of pain as a prerequisite to beginning the journey toward enlightenment. This is a little similar to the Christian prerequisite to confessing one's sins and inner suffering before expressing one's desire to be saved. Only then can the new, born-again individual accept the saving power of Christ.

In the search for what is value and for those values that we hope will bring us happiness, we need to understand what things, values, and behaviors generate joy. But, we also need to be aware of what, within ourselves and/or within our environment, blocks or destroys that happiness for which we so desperately long.

THE VALUE OF DREAMS

Can we dare to dream?

One of the greatest movies produced in the 1930s was *The Wizard of Oz*. Do you remember the yellow brick road? And that timeless song: *Over the Rainbow*?

> Somewhere, over the rainbow, bluebirds fly.
> Somewhere over the rainbow, skies are blue,
> And the dreams that you dare to dream
> Truly do come true.

Shortly after I got married, I started to work like a crazy man in order to support a rapidly growing family. Six or seven years later came a crisis, and I found myself without motivation or desire to go forward. At that time, I didn't feel any support from any quarter. I only worried about getting by, hoping that my old car would not break down and would continue to drag me to work every gray and tiring day through the painful morning traffic. I felt surrounded by a hostile world. I lost hope in the future, in *my* future. Does it sound familiar? What happened was that, after my desires had been so often denied, I started to forget my dreams and aspirations.

We all have, or at an earlier age had, dreams and ideals. We all have a vision of the world as it should be. We all have fantasies about how our life should proceed. We all know that we have gifts and special qualities that should be recognized by others and allow us to give something to our loved ones and to society. Unfortunately, a lot of the hopes and dreams we had when we were younger have not materialized, and, as we get older, those dreams become more distant and finally disappear, replaced only by the cold hardships of everyday life.

As we will notice over and over in this book, human desires are at the root and often the direct cause of human behavior.

Powerful desires are what propel us to make choices, act, and ultimately grow and prosper. Without the inner energy provided by desires, human beings tend to vegetate, and, without healthy dreams, ideals, and a wholesome vision of the future, societies tend to decay, like ancient Greece and imperial Rome. Without vision, goals and projects, a business rusts and stumbles. Without clear objectives and insightful leadership, an army will be defeated (as it happened in Vietnam).

But, there is a silver lining in every cloud. Sometimes, crises in our aspirations may be beneficial because they lead us to a moment of personal scrutiny, where we can pause and analyze the road that we have traveled, where we stand, and where we want to go.

I remember how, in those difficult moments, I felt alone, without solutions, in a blind alley unable to go backward or forward. I felt like nobody could understand me. Nobody cared about my problems or my pains. At the bottom of the pit, I did not even care about my own life. I remember that, at a certain moment, I could not take it anymore. In that one moment, I made a conscious decision: I had had enough! Enough of the pain! So, in a split second (and all real decisions are always made in an instant), I decided to stop being defeated by the pain. I decided to stop rolling over in my painful situation, like a pig rolling in the mud. Yes, the problems would remain, but I was *not* going to feel sorry about them. I was not going to feel sorry for poor old me. I was going to move on.

If I could not reach my prior dreams and goals, if I could not fulfill those desires, fine. I was going to change them. I was not going to be chained by those desires. I was going to find new and more empowering, more reachable desires, and, in fulfilling them, I was going to find some of the joy and satisfaction I needed. It worked beautifully. If you are ever in the pits, try it. It'll also work for you.

In choosing to change ourselves, we need to change our needs and desires. Thus, we change the way we perceive the world and ourselves. We change our behavior, and we change also the world that surrounds us.

Desires lead to choices, but we can also decide to rearrange the desires that are going to move us.

In management studies, a business cycle ends with an evaluation of the program and its results. Normally, today's management styles require a six-step process: 1. Delineate the vision and the purpose of the enterprise. 2. Establish goals and objectives. 3. Determine actors, actions, and programs. 4. Activate the programs. 5. Evaluate the results. 6. Restart the process.

Let us bring strategic planning to our private lives. The important thing to do, particularly during those times when we feel alone, without motivation or vision, is to use profitably this downtime in order to reevaluate our situation and make new and better plans for our future.

At this point, when we make the plan, set the objectives, and identify the major actors who will help us carry on our goals, that's when we are taking a stand. We are making a decision, a choice that will influence our future destiny. Focusing on a decision and a specific project liberates powerful new energies hidden in our minds and hearts. At this point, we begin to regain control of our lives.

Ever notice the pretty girls in scant clothing who advertise beer, exotic travels, or fast cars? One of the first things taught in marketing is how to influence customer behavior. This is the study of the motivations that move people to behave in a certain way (both conscious and unconscious) that will lead them to buy one product instead of another.

Just as marketers, we must understand what motivates us. Nobody knows better than you what it is that moves you. There is nobody better qualified to motivate us than ourselves. Naturally, some people will argue that the environment, circumstances and other factors (our traditions, religion, culture, family, friends, etc.) influence our point of view and, therefore, condition our values, our choices and behavior. All this is true, but we must place these two seemingly conflicting points of view in the right perspective.

Values derive their motivating force both from our own inner psyche as well as from the external environment. There is a binary (and complementary) influence in our motivational make-up: the inner desires spring from the well of our individual character and the external ones that are learned and influenced by our experiences, our environment and our culture and traditions.

THE WAY WE SUFFER

A desire denied makes your heart sick

The General Post Office was a great building, in the heart of downtown. It had very high ceilings, huge doors and windows, and yet it was dark. The stones had been white, but now they had a grayish tint. The big statues, just outside the main entrance, were too somber. Nobody smiled. People, older people with gray clothes and bad breath, always came in just to complain.

Lionel, a postmaster, dreamed of warm, white, sandy beaches, away from everyone and away from it all. But, today he had to deal with really, really, really, nasty people, all day long at the complaint window of the Central Post Office. Now, he feels disgruntled and upset, and he's thinking of maybe grabbing his old M16 rifle and shooting someone. And, that's not just a bad joke.

Joe wants a new car but cannot even afford to fix the old one, so he feels dissatisfied, frustrated, and sad. Caroline always wanted a college education, but she must continue to work as a waitress at the local diner, just to keep a roof over her head.

Harold would like to buy a new dishwasher for Mary, but his boss will not give him a raise, so he feels sad, ashamed, and angry.

Today, psychology has proven that frustration and stress are the great culprits of many psychological as well as physiological disorders, from anxiety to heart problems, gastric ulcers (I know that for a fact), backaches, migraines, etc. Some people escape the frustration and stress of everyday life by going into their fantasy world. Others fall into chronic apathy. Others resort to anger and aggression, and some regress to childish or otherwise immature behaviors.

Frustration and stress are without any doubt the most common pains of contemporary America.

Frustration and unfulfilled desires can make not only your mind sick, but your body as well. The number one killer in the U.S., heart disease, is significantly increased by excessive stress (which may be exacerbated further by having purchased shares of Amazon.com or other dotsters at inflated prices).

Finally, we start to admit that American workers (blue, white or other colored collar) are working longer and harder. What's worse is that their wages are not keeping up with inflation (the real one, the cost of contemporary life) and certainly are not keeping up with the salary increases of top CEO's (from Enron executives to the likes of Walt Disney's Michael Eisner who, in 1994 alone, made over $200 million in bonuses).

Don't get me wrong. I do not endorse socialist ideas of equalizing incomes. There has always been, everywhere, disparity of remuneration, but the problem is with the magnitude of inequality. As the French philosopher (and part-time politician) Voltaire said (just before the head-rolling French Revolution of 1779 that overturned the French Monarchy), "There is nothing wrong with differences in compensation, the evil lies in the disproportionate enormity of the present disparity."

Lots of today's stress and some family breakdowns are related to job-related hopelessness. We cannot escape the affliction of our ever-wanting, irritable, emotional, and greedy nature, but we can try to better understand its workings, the mechanism of how happiness is realized, and the relationship between happiness and the fulfillment of human desires. Let's get technical . . . kind of.

The first type of lack of joy is derived from not having the things we desire. We all know what that means. The second type of lack of joy comes when we are forced to endure something that we do not want or like (Jerry's girlfriend's excessively salivating dog, Michael's mother-in-law staying another week in the house, a long nail in the tire of your brand new car, or a very long list of people and things for most Chinese).

If we were to use a formula, we could say that **happiness** (H) is proportional to the **fulfillment** of man's needs and desires (F) and is inversely proportional to the "quantity" of man's **desires** (D). $H = F/D$, if you will.

In other words, you can increase your happiness by fulfilling more of your desires, by changing or decreasing your wants, or by making your desires more modest and/or achievable.

Modern economic value theories concur in stating that the prices of goods and their values are proportional to the desire of the market for those goods. Of course, this works in our "excessive consumption" society. But, let us assume that there once was a place or a country (some tribe in the Amazon jungle) where people's desires were so limited and their degree of satisfaction so low that they could be happy with very few, simple goods and very little consumption. In that particular market, the so-called contemporary laws of economic value theory would simply not work.

So, reducing one's appetite for excessive and trivial consumption is, without any doubt, one way of reducing frustration, stress and unhappiness. If we can develop the ability to find fulfillment and joy, particularly in those things that are free, such as the beauty of nature, the laughter of children, helping others, etc., then we are on the right road toward a less stressful and fuller life. Sorry, there is nothing much new here. You already knew all this stuff. I just felt good about adding it here.

Desires, particularly extreme desires, can often get you in trouble. Consider the ant that fell in love with the elephant. The ant and the elephant share a night of romance. The next morning the ant wakes up and the elephant is dead. "Damn," says the ant.

"One night of passion and I spend the rest of my life digging a grave!"

What complicates things is that man's desires are not constant, but continue to change, grow, and/or diminish with the passing of time. It is equally true that, if people were to have very few desires or almost none, it would be easier for them to be happy if those little desires were to be fulfilled.

Unfortunately, it is in the search for financial security that we find a tendency for our desires to grow. And, whereas we may think that we will be happy in a $250,000 house, by the time we arrive there, maybe with a family of five, we may find that our desire has grown. Now, we want a much larger dwelling, possibly around $400,000. That nice $40,000 car can be easily replaced by that luxury $80,000 sport convertible. Why?! Don't you want a better, faster computer?! Or a bigger TV?! And, so on and so on.

It is likely that, in the remote, innermost aspects of human nature, his and her emotional and intellectual desires play a similar trick.

So, where and when does it all end? Hopefully, never. Probably nowhere. As long as men and women live, there will always be another dwelling to build, another frontier to cross, another desire to quench. In many different forms, the pursuit of happiness will go on. Our challenge consists of having fun getting there, without complaints, frustration, or remorse.

PRISON

Destroying Desire

If it's true that fulfillment and happiness are connected to desire, it follows that, by eliminating any form of satisfaction and by continually and consistently denying even a partial fulfillment of a person's hopes, their desires will atrophy and eventually die. Without any fulfillment, human drives shrink and wither. At this point, people often withdraw into themselves. Not being able to find anything or anyone with whom to fulfill their emotional needs (like someone placed in jail or a concentration camp), such individuals will usually be left with only the most basic of all desires: staying alive. Have you been to the zoo lately? If you have not met Mr. Greenspan personally, do the next best thing and look at the sad look of most of the zoo's permanent residents.

The survival instinct is certainly the most deeply rooted force in all living creatures. But, it is also true that, if we were to make the situation miserable enough, or if the pain became too great, even that one desire could be drowned in a sea of desperation. One of the reasons for suicide is not that human beings lose their desire for survival, but rather that they have come to a point where the pain associated with their inability to fulfill their desires becomes too great and overpowers their most fundamental life-instinct. In other words, the very moment humans have **no hope** left is when they reach the bottom of their misery.

During the Korean and Vietnam wars, communist experts in torture used psychological and ideological warfare in order to extract information from captured military personnel or, if possible, turn the prisoners into collaborators. Those experts knew how to use the destruction of hope to subdue the human psyche (ask Senator McCain). *The Deer Hunter*, a great movie, with Robert De Niro, was the story of a few friends captured by the Vietcong. There, in the jungle of Vietnam, in the utter hopelessness, desperation and torture of the prison camp, life becomes such a painful experience that death becomes but a welcomed reliever.

At the opposite end, we can see how priests and monks of just about any religion inspire their followers by installing greater and greater hopes into their hearts and minds.

But even positive values like patriotism can quickly degenerate into false and destructive values. We cannot forget the images of the concentration camps brought forth by Nazism or the pseudo-religion that is Communism. Unfortunately, communist ideology is still around, often in disguise, and it is still infecting, like a putrid carcass, the minds and the hearts of many people. Some of them are unaware of its lies, its distorted values, and its enslaving demands to submit one's self to the omnipresent power of the State and to a few individuals knowingly bent on "programming" the minds of the masses according to some weird, nightmarish vision of a utopian society.

To be free means also to reject the false values that bind us to superstition, refute unjust demands, and refuse to be defeated by whatever adversities and whatever scorn, sneers and pain the old "paradigm" may decide to lay down on us.

Some Western students of Buddhism have translated the quest for nirvana as the absence of passion and the extinguishments of all forms of desire. This is completely false, since Buddhism does not teach the elimination of desires but rather training the human mind to control and guide the passions that flourish in the human heart. A Buddhist proverb says that it is easier to tame a wild tiger than to tame one's own emotions, particularly anger and fear.

Anger and fear block communication. Fear can freeze one's mind and body. Angry people very often fail to hear what others have to say. And, whatever they hear, they are likely to put the worst possible interpretation on both the words and actions of whoever is seen as an adversary. Anger (hate) and fear are the dominant emotions of any dictatorship. Over them reign supreme superstition, ignorance, oppression, and a host of other hellish moods, while true reason (wisdom) is scorned and repressed.

I had many long talks by our swimming pool with Danny Abraham (former owner of Slimfast Corporation), a fine gentleman, deeply devoted to Israel, and dedicated to bring peace to the region. Unfortunately, I believe that the Middle East will likely continue to be a crucible of anger, fear, blood, and tears. Number one reason: because most people are not willing or able to control their emotions. If we want to affect what is going on around us, if we want to influence the way others behave, we must be aware of emotions and motivations that may be stirring their hearts and clouding their minds. Especially when we try to communicate with an opposing party, we must be more concerned with their feelings and their assumptions (feelings that are likely to distort our rational arguments) than with our desire to succeed.

Going back to the Bible story of Abraham, Isaac and Ishmael, we can note the emotional nature of the conflict between Abraham's first wife, Sarah, and his second wife, Agar. If the two women were still alive today, it may be easier to make peace between the Israelis and the Palestinians than trying to get these two ladies to reconcile.

Life is full of challenges to overcome, tests, and temptations not to be fallen into. Temptation is just the hard way to learn. If we do not fall into it, we learn without having to pay the price. And to those who ask "How do we learn unless we try?" I answer that we can easily resist the temptation to slam into a brick wall at 60 miles an hour without having to try it to learn it the hard way.

We can and we must become makers and drivers of our own dreams, knitting our own future, and not falling, like a moth (or like gullible pawns of communist propaganda) into the consuming flames of hate, violence and false promises of an illusory paradise.

TIBET

Finding Purpose

It was cold. The snow was wet, freezing, and dirty. Even at noon, the sky was a dark, chilly shade of gray. Nothing like the images Frank had seen in the Happy Trails travel office in Jersey City a few weeks earlier. The real Nepal had nothing in common with what he had imagined.

As Frank sat on a pile of uncomfortable rocks, considering the possibility of an earlier flight home, a young monk in the traditional orange robe approached him and asked, "You tired to stay here?" The monk, with slightly crossed eyes, kept staring at him, then went on to speak in a broken English that made Frank wonder where the monk could have possibly learned it from. "The answers you looking cannot be found in one place. You must know *why* you want to know."

Frank had a flash of insight. "That's it," thought Frank. "That is the right question!" Having studied a short course on strategic planning in college, Frank had a moment of enlightenment. His teacher of economics at NYU used to say, "When you cannot see clearly, ask yourself—why am I doing this? What's my purpose?" Frank took an early plane home. He gladly paid the surcharge, and, while landing at JFK International Airport, he felt really good about his short voyage of inner discovery.

But, unlike Frank, Ricky Martin or the Beatles, most of us never went to Nepal or Tibet. But, some of us did search, at least for a while, for the answers to age-old questions. And, almost all of us have checked, even if for a moment, into religion for answers. But religions themselves need a reason d'etre, a purpose.

What is the purpose of religion? In a simplistic way, we could say that the purpose of religion is to fulfill a spiritual, emotional, moral, and sometimes mental need of the people. Having said that, let me make perfectly clear that I do *NOT* agree at all with Karl Marx's definition of religions as the "opium of the masses" (opium is the old name for the drug heroin for those few innocent souls who did not know).

Rather, religion is something that relates to the deepest, most noble and valuable aspect of human nature and beliefs, even if, at times, some people (such as a certain Ayatollah of a few years back) carry the consequences of their faith and beliefs a bit too far, denying to others the freedom to differ in their beliefs and values.

On the seemingly opposite side, the purpose of the study of economics is clearly to understand the way human beings interact with commodities, with products, and with each other in order to fulfill those material and physiological needs (food, clothing, shelter, etc.) to which we were referring before.

The goal, in both cases, is somewhat similar because the ultimate purpose of both religion and economics is the pursuit of one's happiness. In a superficial way, we could say that, in the religious sphere, man searches for some kind of inner joy and spiritual fulfillment. In the economic sphere, man seeks to find a more material satisfaction and well-being. Thus, we are again full circle to the two kinds of desires (binary, if you like); the first is for inner fulfillment and happiness, while the second is for external fulfillment, joy, and pleasure.

Spain's Prime Minister, Jose Maria Aznar (left)
with Mr. Lombardi (right)

The President of the Italian Senate, Mr. Marello Pera (left)
with Mr. Lombardi

Mr. Lombardi (left) with former French President
Valery Gisgard d'Estaing (right)

Mr. Lombardi (left) has kept a close working relationship with
some of the most influential reformers of the Italian Government,
such as Mr. Guilio Tremonti, Minister of Finance (right), and
Mr. Umberto Bossi, Minister of Constitutional Reform (center).

Mr. Lombardi (right) presented a copy of his previous book *Liberta' e Progresso Economico (Freedom and Economic Progress)* to His Holiness Pope John Paul II

A great admirer of His Holiness and the Dalai Lama, Mr. Lombardi has studied Tibetan Buddhism for two decades, and met the Dalai Lama (left) in several occasions, seeking a modern interpretation of the meaning of the *Two Truths*.

FROM DESIRES TO BELIEFS

What do you believe?

The Pyramids of ancient Egypt have always inspired a sense of mystery and awe. From those imposing pyramids to the high terraces of the Mayan temples in Central America, whenever humans felt that somehow the sun was the giver of life, they came to value it and even worship it as a visible expression of some perceived higher force, erecting monuments to a divine power they believed came through its warmth and light.

When, in our early history, men learned that little seeds of wheat and corn could be used to grow more corn and wheat, they came to value the seeds as well as the knowledge of how to best make them grow. When men and women valued large families and lots of children, they performed fertility rites and created belief systems, some more or less correct, centered on their perceived needs and limited knowledge. There is no doubt that the way we perceive reality helps shape our evaluation of it; thus, perceptions, beliefs and values interconnect.

Since time immemorial the world over, among all deeply held beliefs, undoubtedly the strongest ones have always been about faith and religion. Recent polls showed that 93% of Americans believe in God or some superior being, 82% believe in some form or another of after-life, and 64% believe in the need to tolerate other people's religious beliefs.

Beliefs, both those based on real facts and those based on superstition or incomplete and erroneous information (i.e., beliefs founded on a correct perception of reality and those based on erroneous assumptions), have a great influence on our attitudes and values.

Thus, people often come to value those things that, within the reality of the natural world as they experience it, help them fulfill their needs, desires, and dreams. Those things help to contribute to the well-being of the individual and/or the community. But beliefs change. When the physical conditions under which the group's life takes place change, or when social, religious, or technological developments reshape the old belief system, then we see a reshaping of the common values as a form of "social evolution" continues to move forward.

What we believe, how we see the world in which we live, and our "world view" is often the very ground upon which we build our beliefs and value system. Generally speaking, our deepest beliefs lead us to draw conclusions concerning people and situations. Different worldviews will produce different value systems and, therefore, different behaviors. We may prioritize *doing* instead of *being*. We may give greater importance to *individualism or collectivism*. We may view the world as an exciting, challenging place or as dangerous and full of conflict. Our beliefs (valid or not) will influence our attitudes and our actions.

Some people think that events control our lives, that the environment shapes our character. Not true. I'll spare you the story of the two brothers with an alcoholic father, one who became a criminal, and one who became a priest. Or the story of the two POW's tortured in Vietnam, one caved in (and was then killed) while the other never surrendered (and became a Senator).

Personal beliefs are generalized interpretations of our past experiences (conscious and un-conscious). They are a sort of "perceived" cause-effect phenomena based on a personal interpretation of events. The more the experience is repeated or reinforced by others (family, friends, authority figures), the more it becomes radicated.

We are the ones that give meaning to events and experiences. What we believe our experiences *mean* to us is what shapes our attitude and our behavior.

A belief is an act of will, a conscious or un-conscious decision that influences our values, norms, and traditions. Sometimes,

114

we may repeat over and over again in our minds an event and our interpretation of that event (an accident, a time when we got hurt, a time when we were humiliated), until we reach the point of becoming obsessed by it.

We often choose to adopt beliefs from other meaningful people (family, friends, coworkers, people in authority, the omnipresent TV networks) even without our personal experience of them; with repetition (unfortunately), we become more convinced of their validity.

Human beings have the great ability to create meaning. In giving meaning to events, we give power to (or dis-empower) them.

Beliefs greatly influence how we feel and what we do. However, there are different levels of belief that have different levels of impact on the decisions we make. All beliefs are essentially cultural; in the sense that they can be learned, they can be the result of personal experiences or can be transmitted by family, traditions, and society.

And, just as we distinguish between two very unique kinds of perceptions, me and the world, we can distinguish between two basic kinds of beliefs. The first is about ourselves—how we "see" ourselves, our image of what and who we are. The second belief is about our perception of the external world and other people.

So, from these two "inborn" perceptions (me-world), we derive two essential kinds of belief. The first set of beliefs is about ourselves, our self-identity, and our self-worth; the second set concerns how we "see" others and the world.

Some psychologists have said that the most powerful belief is our own sense of identity, and that *this* is the ultimate filter of all of our perceptions. There is no doubt that beliefs about one's self are primary. Very often, changes in the way we perceive and value ourselves cause changes in the way we perceive and value others, and this often leads us to change our value-system as well as our behavior.

We make choices, and we act as a function of who we are and

how we see ourselves. These "inner" beliefs (conscious and unconscious) are very important because they are the beliefs that we use to define our own individuality; it is that which makes us unique and different from other individuals. This certainty about who we are and what we are capable or not capable of doing most often creates the boundaries and limits within which we behave.

In the Marines and Special Forces, training is equally divided between the body and the mind.

Just like the ancient Romans (most notable a group called the "Stoics," who followed a strict discipline of body and mind), many, from martial arts practitioners to Greek Orthodox monks, have learned the importance of disciplining one's mind (and emotions, I would add) in order to better command one's body and overcome its limitations.

We have often been told, and today's science has proven it, that human potential is a lot greater than what we actually use, and that much of the potential we use depends upon the conception that we have about ourselves: our self-identity.

Actions follow beliefs and values, and most people (driven by their rational brain's need for consistency and coherence) act consistently with their views of who they are, whether that view is accurate or not.

The beliefs about ourselves are primary in the sense that they often influence our beliefs about others and our relationship to the world.

It is only after we have established a basic self-identity that we know who we are in relationship to others and can decide how to relate to others and what to do (how to make choices).

Then, we start to formulate values. We adopt or reject other beliefs, and we establish or reject rules and traditions. Finally, we judge whether something is good, bad or indifferent. Of course, the baby that judged mother's-milk-good, or spanking-doctor-bad, skipped some of these steps and had his needs and his intuition do the judging.

One of the most important discoveries made by social

scientists and behaviorists in the last two decades has been the correlation between self-identity and behavior. Namely, changes in one's self-identity lead to behavioral changes. As the individual develops new beliefs about who he or she is, his or her behavior changes in accordance with the new identity. At this point, we need to add something equally important.

Just as we have organized the categories of human perception into a binary set—the self and the world or the one and the many—we can also identify and distinguish between two essential sets of beliefs: those dealing with the individual self, and those dealing with the community and the world at large. Applying these categories to behavioral science, we arrive at another equally important conclusion.

Just as changes in the perception of one's self (in the self-identity of an individual) bring about changes in one's value-system and subsequently in one's behavior, so do changes in the self-identity of a group lead to changes in its behavior towards its own members and towards other communities.

As a community of people (an ethnic group, a Nation, a family, a society) changes its perception of its own identity and develops new beliefs about its self-identity and its perceived relationship to other communities (Iran before and after the Shah, Yugoslavia before and after Milosovich), so will its values reflect the shift towards the new identity. This will change its behavior towards other communities and towards its own people (its culture, traditions and social rules).

There are few forces more potent and able to leverage and shape human behavior than self-identity, be it individual self-identity or the self-identity of the community within which the individual identifies himself. As an exercise, try to make use of this important tool to modify your behavior.

Someone might ask, "How can I change myself if I never had certain positive experiences?" The answer is that self-identity is NOT limited to our experience. Rather, *only our interpretation of our experiences limits our perception of who we are.*

Our identity is determined by both our decisions about who

we are and the labels we decide to identify with. The way we define our identity also defines our way of life. Just as there are elements of our "DNA" in the choices we make and which determine our behavior, there are other inborn elements also in our experiences and in our interpretation of them (experiences might be significant events in our life, both positive and negative). In addition, we consciously and subconsciously define our self-identity based on what other people have told us about ourselves.

In conclusion, we can find an answer that is in tune with our relational approach. Self-identity can be produced by two complementary and inter-related elements: 1. From the inborn sense of "self" (the "one") that is derived from our genetic make-up, and 2. From the totality of conscious and subconscious experiences (our relationship with the world, the "many") and our very unique *interpretation* (our choices) of them. Having examined one binary aspect of desires and value, external and internal, we can now look at another binary, or relational, set of desires: personal desires and communal desires; that is, desires for the benefit of the self (the single individual) and desires for the well-being of the many (the community of which the individual is part).

DARWIN, ADAM SMITH, AND RUSSELL CROWE

Individual and group well being

Going back to the prehistoric cave men that Darwin was so fond of, we could come to the apparent conclusion that altruism results from the social evolutionary process of selection, whereby groups are advantaged if they contain members who are willing to sacrifice themselves for the group. Charles Darwin wrote in *The Descent of Man:*

> *When two tribes came into competition, and if*

> *one tribe was composed of self-centered individuals interested only in their own personal safety, while one tribe included a great number of courageous, sympathetic and faithful members, who were always ready to warn each other of danger, to aid and defend each other, this tribe would succeed better than the other.*

In such a case, the values of courage, sympathy, and faithfulness seem to be "selected" by the evolutionary process. At any rate, it is clear that a group of purely self-serving individuals is bound for extinction. Helping others in one's community or group is not only an inborn self-preserving instinct, it is also a power exchange that gives back value to the helper.

Even when the helping behavior is due to more selfless reasons, argues Darwin, there is a byproduct whereby "the donor has augmented his or her power while the recipient forfeits some power." This fact may help explain why the common saying that "No good deed ever goes unrewarded" (or a bad deed unpunished) has some truth to it. Indeed, the recipient, who may end up disliking the helper because he or she senses intuitively that they lost something, does not always receive helping with gratitude and warmth, but this fact does not change the equation.

Thus, people don't want to be *given* justice, for example, so much as they want to take an effective and meaningful part in the dialogue that produces it. Yet, cynical witticism notwithstanding, for most people most of the time, one good deed deserves another, and reciprocity often wins the day.

In a scene from the movie, *A Beautiful Mind*, the main character, John Forbes Nash, portrayed by Russell Crowe, has a flash of insight when he tries to explain to his fellow classmates how Adam Smith's statement that "greater value is found when individuals find ways to serve the community's needs before one's own" can be improved by the rule that states that "an even greater value is found when individuals find activities that can serve both the individual as well as the community."

Very often, an individual's personal well-being is consistent with the well-being of the group, especially from a broad, long-term perspective. Thus, some behavior may be egoistic and altruistic at the same time. It is, in many instances, perfectly moral to do what is in your own best interest, not only for your own good but for the good of others as well.

Here, we see how Adam Smith's seemingly contradictory statements find substance. For example, you may want to go to a motion picture or to the beach, rather than go to work as you are supposed to. But, you go to work because you need your job and want to continue eating and paying your rent. You did the right thing, the moral thing, both in light of your own long-term best interests and your obligations to society. Of course, if you really, really want to go to the beach, go ahead. You can always get another job, maybe flipping hamburgers.

When personal well-being and society's (or the company you work for) well-being collide, as they must on occasion, then the situation invites analysis. First, do they really collide? What action contributes to your personal well-being in a given case in the long run? Is society's welfare being served or not by your acts? Second, if an apparent conflict continues to arise, is it because of an actual conflict between the underlying values of the individual versus the values of the community—or is it only a matter of the desire of the individual to do something that is not contemplated, at that particular time and under those circumstances, by that society?

Certain acts of rebellion sometimes reflect the very need of the community to change and grow. Just like during puberty and adolescence, the individual's need to assert his/her individual rights and freedoms may temporarily clash with the rules of the parents and the family. Similarly, societies and civilizations go through stages of growth. But the needs and desires of the new generation are essential to the further growth of the family and the development of the community. In this sense, some rebellions (like the American Revolution of 1776 and the French Revolution a few years later) can be considered positive changes in the growth processes of their respective societies.

Some of our positive values, such as cooperation, sharing, unity and even compassion may have more to do with the structure of human society than with some "nobleness" in our nature. On the other hand, if we watch too much television, particularly some cynical and pessimistic propaganda disguised as so-called news, it seems that greed, pride, dishonesty, covetousness, cowardice, lust, wrath, gluttony, envy, thievery, promiscuity, stubbornness, selfishness, egocentrism, and disobedience, among many other human dispositions, constantly threaten the survival or well-being of our society. But the truth is that even if these attitudes seem widespread, they are as universal as are our constant efforts to control them. Just like these stances had a sort of positive survival value once, long ago, starting in our prehistoric past, so as society progress, they become a hindrance to the welfare of the community.

Just like a newborn who cares only for his feeding, and a young child who cares primarily for his or her selfish needs and desires, this self-centeredness and lack of consideration for others is due to an inborn, and therefore natural mechanism of self-preservation. Only later, with adolescence, do young men and women start to be concerned with the welfare of others.

Similarly, in the development of human society through history, we notice a gradual change in social values, from more selfish values needed for physical survival, to more inclusive and communal values geared to the growth, progress and well-being not only of the individual but of the larger community. With the development of society, the more egocentric values became obstacles to the cooperation necessary to carry on orderly community life, especially large-scale, complex community life. In no advanced society do parents teach their children to be selfish, greedy, angry, stubborn, envious, or disobedient; instead, they often search for means to limit or eliminate these characteristics in their children. Unfortunately, there are still many aspects of society that force us into adopting the "law of the jungle" as the best rule for surviving and prospering.

Some scholars have stated that, "The persistence of a society depends on its ability to provide adequate social mechanisms (and the values they represent): 1. for the production, distribution, and consumption of goods and services; 2. for the social control, supervision, and coordination of its members through laws and authority systems; 3. for the health and physical care of its members; 4. for the education and training of children to occupy adult roles and for children's socialization into the society; 5. for the justification of the society's core beliefs, values, and ways of behaving (be it scientific or religious); 6. for recreation and play; and 7. for the allocation of adult roles (e.g., the division of labor) and for the conferral of status among its members."

Societies, of course, are diverse in how they perform these functions, and that depends, at least in part, on how well each is legitimated by moral codes, and by accepted values (and by how good and wise their political leaders are).

This means that every living person has duties and obligations to others according to the age, sex, and other social roles he or she occupies. Every living person experiences changes in such social roles throughout life (e.g., from young to old), has social ties of kinship to other people, learns from others, is rewarded or punished according to the presumed rightness or wrongness of his or her behavior, has certain rights, and so on. Most of our communal values are derived from the necessity of the group to exalt communal values above selfish ones for the very survival of the group. Sharing with others within a closely-knit group (just like some teenagers) was a key value and behavior pattern in small-scale societies, especially among hunting and gathering and rudimentary farming societies, when life was hazardous and successful outcomes of individual efforts were dicey. Without such values as sharing and reciprocity, and the redistribution of foodstuffs among group members, many individuals, and possibly the group itself, would not survive.

Social scientists tell us that another very important value that evolves in the life of a child to that of an adult is the value of trust. Trust is of particular importance in maintaining a healthy community life. This applies particularly well to the financial community. When trust in an institution falls, its financial value falls as well. When trust in the value of stocks weakens, the stock market collapses (as we have witness all too well in 2001 and 2002). For a community to work effectively, there is a trust that deals with expectations of others as being technically competent. And there is a trust concerning expectations that people will fulfill their direct moral responsibilities for the welfare of others (of special interest may be the bonds of mutual trust that develop within a military unit), from the trust of people who direct the traffic, to those who enforce the law, to the millions that drive everyday to work who we trust will stay on their side of an undivided highway.

And yet, somehow, distrust can also be useful for the maintenance of social order. For example, rationally based expectations that someone will not carry out a technically competent performance or will deliberately fail to fulfill an obligation can be beneficial, both by preventing one's exploitation and, more importantly, by motivating action to create mechanisms of social control, like the fire fighters or the police.

To paraphrase Archimedes, the fifth century B.C. mathematician, "Give me a lever and a place to stand on, and I will lift the earth." The power of human values and the understanding of their workings are like a lever that increases people's ability to accomplish their goals. By offering new tools to manage change, it is possible to help people tackle all kinds of problems and opportunities with greater effectiveness.

The fulcrum I like to use is the new value matrix, a new binary system of valuation, and the multiple interconnected opportunities for constructive change that it offers its users.

THE MATRIX . . . AGAIN

Binary Choices, Binary Values

Returning to our binary matrix and the basic concept of the individual and the community, we can distinguish between the needs and choices of the individual and those that are common to an entire community.

Sometimes, the needs of the individual coincide with those of the community (e.g., the need for a healthy environment, sufficient nutrition, an appropriate transportation system), but, on other occasions, the self-centered desires of the individual can be in conflict with the norms and parameters established by the community (e.g., speed limits on the roads, zoning laws, etc.).

Just as goals can be divided into two categories (individual and collective), human choices can also be divided between those that are made by the community and those that are made by the individual. Consequently, objects and/or people and situations can be found to have "value", either for just one individual or for a group of individuals (a community).

Goals
→ Collective goals
→ Individual goals

Choices
→ Collective choices
→ Individual choices

Values
→ Collective values
→ Individual values

In this context, it is interesting to note that it is practically impossible to foresee the outcome of choices made by individuals. That's because the parameters used for making these judgments are peculiar to the heart and mind of each individual, and because they are entirely subjective and can be affected by temporary changes in the psychological, social, and cultural situation of that individual. It is easier to anticipate the choices and changes relating to the community. In this second case, it is even possible to make statistical calculations on the community's reactions to a given situation.

Strictly speaking, individual choices are not entirely subjective, otherwise, it would also be impossible to reach statistical probability for a group of people who are all acting in an entirely subjective manner. There is some degree of objective predictability even for an isolated individual action, but it is, of course, much lower than for a group where the unpredictable factor linked to human freedom is balanced out by the large number.

Additionally, we have already divided our desires and needs (and the values associated with them) into another set of categories: needs and desires that are of an external, material nature versus those that have a more inner, intangible nature.

Desires
→ External/material
→ Internal/intangible

Needs
→ External/material (physiological)
→ Internal (psychological, emotional, mental)

To each of these categories of needs and desires correspond values that can also be classified as external/material values and inner/intangible values.

Values
→ External/material
→ Internal/intangible

Material values linked to material (physical) desires, especially those pertaining to basic human needs (air, food, shelter, clothing, health), are rather easy to pinpoint and predict. However, some of the less essential needs (fashion, home furnishing, types of entertainment, etc.) can be anticipated with a relatively lower level of accuracy. This is also the case when calculating the priority of communal values of a psychological or inner nature (love, freedom, compassion, democracy, justice, happiness). It is only when dealing with an individual's values of a conceptual, emotional, or mental nature that we experience great difficulty in making predictions, since judgments on these values vary from individual to individual and even from moment to moment.

The fundamental psychological nature of a human being cannot be changed, just as it is not possible to change our basic bodily functions (such as breathing or eating). Nor can we change the inborn functions of our brain without destroying our entire organism. As a result, we can say that some of the basic material values, such as oxygen or food—and also internal values, such as beauty, justice, freedom, peace, love and others—will always remain unchanged, regardless of culture or religious beliefs. These values will not be affected by historical events, because they are derived from the deepest levels of our human nature and consciousness. Such values should, therefore, be the very foundation of a worldwide and globally accepted system of values (be they moral or material). This should then lead to a global economy with a similar universal appeal. The development of such a system should be the very first goal of any future theory of value.

A GOOD MAN ALWAYS KNOWS HIS LIMITATIONS

I wish Greenspan did

Unceremoniously dropping the bomb that was intended for him in the bad guy's car, Inspector Callahan, also known as "Dirty Harry," in the final scene of *Magnum Force,* starring Clint

Eastwood, slowly utters the famous warning: "A good man always knows his limitations."

But, unlike Inspector Callahan, many economists and other dogmatists seem to believe themselves infallible. In most cases, national economies and economic dogmas are founded on their predominant ideological tradition. Materialism, for example, represents an omnipresent reality in the entire Western world and in much of the Orient as well. It is present in developed countries and in developing ones. All this, of course, inevitably affects the economic system of these countries.

Yet, even in our materialistic culture, most individuals have non-material desires and, therefore, find values that are non-material and non-monetary. The teacher, the scientist, the preacher, the poet, the artist, the fireman, and the philosopher all unite against the cold, economic "theories" and insist on the joy of giving without reward, on the joy of creating for its own sake, and in helping people in distress because of one's own sense of righteousness.

Human beings are able to find unlimited resources and creativity within themselves, often without need for reward or remuneration. We all admire selfless giving and people like Mother Theresa. We enjoy Jimmy Stewart in movies like *It's a Wonderful Life*. We may cry watching Charles Dickens' *A Christmas Carol*, because we all have (some more, other less) some of those emotions within ourselves.

The way human beings perceive reality does not derive exclusively from external stimuli but also from the interpretation which our thoughts, emotions and prior experiences make of those perceptions. The ability to choose is not derived from the external environment alone, but rather it is the primary quality of the human spirit and thought. The ability to choose is grounded in freedom, and freedom of the individual and liberty of the community is, in my opinion, the primary aspect and very essence of human beings.

All the propaganda done for decades in countries like Cuba, North Korea, China or Russia crumbles in a few days of rebellion, when the masses understand that they already have at their disposal the most formidable weapons in the world: the ability to choose their own destiny, their awareness of already being free, and the ability to change their own economic and political situation (as has taken place, in recent years, in Poland, in Hungary, in the former Czechoslovakia, and in other nations).

Maybe also in Italy, where sometimes I work as a political and organizational consultant, change will become possible. But, change will happen when people have the courage to make the appropriate choices and free themselves from centuries of stagnation, corruption, superstitious traditions, and outdated worldviews.

As someone wrote: *"Mourn not for the dead, but for the apathetic mass, the cowards and the weak, who see the world's evils (and their own) and anguish, but dare not speak or act."*

In order to make lasting changes on those outdated traditions and values, people (from Italy to Argentina to Afghanistan) will need to have a clearer understanding of what values are lasting and empowering, and which ones are based on false assumptions, false beliefs, and outdated traditions.

FROM DESIRE TO VALUE

The Definition

Elizabeth was 15 years old. She loved flowers, all kinds of flowers—big, small, colorful, perfumed, and delicate, delightful flowers. Her heart's desire was to lose herself in the delicious smell of flowers, instead of the stench of the exhaust pipes of her brother's racing car. "Dad," she screamed from her room. "If Kevin doesn't stop revving that engine, I'm gonna kill him!" Then her thoughts went to Charlie, her would-be boyfriend. "If Charlie brings me a dozen roses," she thought, "my desire and my thirst will be satisfied, and I may finally express my happiness with a hug and a long, big kiss." Needless to say, unlike Elizabeth, Kevin loved the smell of oil, glycerin and gas coming from his powerful V8 engine. Different things have different values to different people. So, what is value?

The dictionary tells us that the word VALUE is derived from Latin, from the verb *valere* which means to be worth, to be of valor. *Valuta*, also from Latin, came to indicate any sort of coin or other means of exchange. Economic *Value* first appeared in the 14th Century as: 1. a fair return or equivalent in goods, services, or money for something exchanged; 2. the monetary worth of something, a marketable price; 3. relative worth, utility, or importance. But value is also 4. a numerical quantity that is assigned or is determined by calculation or measurement, 5. as a verb: to estimate or assign the monetary worth, 6. to rate or scale in usefulness, importance, or general worth, 7. the relative duration of a musical note, <a good ~ at the price>, <the ~ of base stealing in baseball >, and so on.

When we find something that satisfies our desires, we find a thing of value. The greater the desire fulfilled, the greater the value. (By the way, did you buy a lottery ticket this week?) Similarly, if we have an expectation for one thing and we receive something that might be its opposite, or that might frustrate our desire, we are likely to express our dissatisfaction and anger. In the first case, the flowers have value since they fulfill Elizabeth's desire. In the second case, the stink of exhaust pipes, like the smell of a dead fish, will have zero or negative value for her.

So, what determines value? The individual does. The individual's needs, his mind and heart's desire determine value (unlike Karl Marx's foolish notion that value is determined by the amount of labor spent to produce an object).

What comes first, the individual's desire or the fulfillment of that desire? Obviously, the desire comes first, and, of course, there must first be an individual who has, feels, and produces that desire. We could even say that there is a relationship of cause and effect between the desire of the individual and the realization of value.

Let's talk, briefly (or I might get in trouble), about the relationship between men and women. If the subject of the study is a man, his desire may be to find the woman of his dreams, a woman who will satisfy most, if not all, of his needs and wants. When he finds such a woman, she will have great value, a value proportional to the extent that she is able to satisfy his wishes.

Naturally, since the woman has some needs and wants of her own, she will look to the man for his ability to fulfill what she perceives are her essential needs. For the man, those qualities or values may be tenderness, patience, understanding, love, trust, a great body, etc. For the woman, those qualities may also be tenderness, patience and understanding, a great body, etc. But, she will probably require, among other things, that the man also be a good provider.

While physiological desires are somehow limited in form and in time (with the possible exclusion of sex, at least among some segments of the Italian population), our internal desires have a tendency to grow and continue. Understanding this difference means understanding how the different kinds of fulfillment, and therefore happiness, are produced.

If we understand the principle of how to satisfy man's desire for happiness, the value matrix, we will also understand the deepest workings of religion and economics. It is not a secret that some of the best marketing gurus could have done just as well promoting religion (like some televangelists have shown all too clearly).

That is not to say that sometimes, human desires can get out of control, like driving faster than the speed limit (got any speed ticket lately?). But, most of the time, they can be rationalized and contained (I know you didn't cry when they towed away your car!). It only means that we must try to understand the basic nature of human desires and values.

In conclusion, someone's desire determines the value of an object, the value of an activity, or the value of an emotion or a concept.

Value is then just an attribute, a quality of an object (any object, person or thing) that somehow fulfills the needs, wants, or desires of an individual. This is what could be called a binary or relational definition of what is value.

VALUE IS THAT QUALITY OF AN OBJECT (E.G., A FLOWER'S PERFUME) THAT SATISFIES THE NEEDS OR DESIRES OF AN INDIVIDUAL (OR A GROUP).

Values are those qualities, characteristics, and "labels" that we give to objects (concrete or abstract) and people in order to indicate the degree to which these objects and people satisfy our needs and desires.

The origin of value is derived from the needs, desires, and the purpose of the individual or the group.

To simplify our investigation into the origin of value, we can classify desires (and therefore the *values* associated with them) into two groups: 1. Individual desires, producing a hierarchy of values for that individual, and 2. Group or collective needs and desires producing collective values.

We may also distinguish between tangible values (material needs and desires, producing material values) and intangible ones (inner needs and desires, generating abstract, conceptual, and emotional values).

Naturally, there are many cases in which human needs and wants are formed by a combination of the two. For example, an infant's desire to communicate can be seen as having both characteristics: a material need to exchange vital information (crying for food or to express discomfort), as well as an inner need to assert his or her individuality (or a desire to receive love and attention).

So, having first separated intangible from material desires (and values), it is now necessary to reunite them, since both are but an aspect of the same reality, the proverbial two faces of the same coin.

The key is to understand their binary nature, as well as the fact that one is but a reflection of the other, and that the best thing to do is try to balance them both equally.

DESIRES LEAD TO VALUES, VALUES LEAD TO CHOICES, And CHOICES LEAD TO BEHAVIOR.

Like a spider on a web, we are the makers of our own destiny. Or, like a butterfly caught in the spider's web, are we the victims of fate? Do we make our own choices, or are choices imposed on us?

CHOICES TURN INTO ACTIONS

Choices determine behavior

From beliefs and values, we arrive at choices. And, that's a problem! How do we choose?

Choose one Friday night date instead of another, and your life may never be the same (for good or for worse). Choose to study at your local Community College rather than going to work at your uncle's gas station, and your life will change. Choose to speed through that red light . . . and your life may change . . . drastically.

So, how do we choose? And why, sometimes, do we feel that whatever the heck we choose does not seem to matter anyway?

Most of us feel powerless when it comes to social issues and world events. We feel perplexed by violent crimes, wars, government inefficiencies, illnesses, death, taxes, etc. We feel we can do so little to influence our society or the world. Unfortunately, these feelings of helplessness may cripple our ability to take action and often prevent us from changing our lives.

When this malaise permeates a whole society, we see the stagnation and even the collapse of a civilization (like Western Europe during the Middle Ages).

The fragmentation of national markets the world over, including the U.S., has created pockets of wealth and pockets of poverty. These pockets will continue to be formed, grow and/or decrease depending on the CHOICES that those communities will make. The major choices made 10 years ago regarding investments in technology are bringing their fruits today, from

Silicon Valley to Washington State, from local counties to entire regions.

In Europe, a small country like Slovenia has gone from a low level economy (before its separation from Yugoslavia) to a wealthier and more civilized form of economic development, thanks to the enlightened choices its leaders and its citizens have made. The same cannot be said for Iraq.

Choices are not the exclusive privilege of the wealthier or more educated communities, quite the opposite. Good, bad, and really stupid choices can be made by anyone, anytime, anywhere (I bet you knew that from personal experience).

The right choices being made in some small communities of India (always regarding investments in new tech and in people-empowering policies) will give them profitable fruits in a short time.

This is the upcoming economic trend: pocket-economy, or as we would say in Italian, "leopard-spotted", techno-economic development.

When individuals discover that they have the ability to change parts of their value system, they find the power to change their own destiny. Similarly, when a society, a nation, or an ethnic community discovers its ability to form a new self-identity and creates a new value system, the destiny of that community changes. This has been the case in Iran, in Serbia, in Afghanistan, and hopefully will be the case in Iraq and Palestine.

What determines the quality of life of the community, the nation, and even the world is connected to the collective decisions we make today and how we deal with present challenges.

Just as a man and a woman create their own destiny by the choices they make, so do communities and nations seal their destinies by the total choices made.

We must understand that *choice is cumulative.* The life we experience is often the result of the sum of a host of choices we have made. Naturally, there are some choices that are more important than others, but the final results are most often a combination of many, seemingly small, individual choices.

Some choices are conscious; others are subconscious. The decision to leave our choice to others is, in itself, a choice to delegate (like a Power of Attorney), and this, too, can be conscious or subconscious.

Similarly, a choice not to choose or not to act, like the choice to remain perfectly still when confronted with a hissing rattlesnake, for example, can be a perfectly natural choice. I wonder why my subconscious has suggested the example of the snake right after I was speaking of attorneys?!

This is why human beings (empowered by nature) tend to remain immobile when confronted with a great or unexpected danger. It is a natural defense mechanism, just as, in the primordial jungle, it was a natural defense mechanism to scream in order to frighten the animal (a wolf or a bear) one unexpectedly encountered in the woods (though this defense does not work with attorneys).

Also, the fear of the dark might be the result of long-lasting memories, passed on in our genes (a kind of collective mind, if you like the psychology of Young), from our ancestors who spent endless nights scrutinizing the dark for dangerous animals. Those animals grew even more fearsome in their fantasies (like in any child's imagination . . . and mine, right after I watched the movie *Alien*).

In conclusion, our choices, our successes or our failures, are not always the result of dramatic, earth-shaking events; rather, they are determined by the sum of the decisions we make and the actions or inactions that follow.

Similarly, in society, the solutions to the great problems (like drugs, teenage pregnancy, or even poverty) are found in gradual behavioral changes and the multitude of decisions involved in that change.

Teenage pregnancy is the direct result of a specific behavior, and that behavior is determined by choices, which, in turn, are influenced by specific values, beliefs, and ultimately by the perception of one's self-identity. Therefore, the key to the solution of the problem of teenage pregnancy can be found primarily in modifying the values, the beliefs, and the self-identity perceptions of the teenagers involved.

In Kosovo and in Albania (another bad situation), as long as its citizens perceived themselves as powerless against a ruthless dictator, nothing changed for decades. Today, those conditions have changed, but, most importantly, the people's perception of themselves, specifically their perception of their right to be free and in control of their own lives, is what has turned the destiny of that community towards a different future (though, alas, not necessarily a better one, considering their aggressive behavior and their desire to dominate narco-traffic and organized crime in the Balkans and in some regions of Italy).

FREEDOM OF CHOICE . . . REALLY?

To thine own self be true

High in the snow-covered forests of the old West, a solitary figure on horseback sings a ballad about a man who became a legend. "The day that you wonder is the day that you choose . . ." So goes the title song of *Jeremiah Johnson*, a great movie and a tribute to freedom. The song continues, " . . . A man will always wonder where the fair wind blows."

Similarly, many of us have learned that what really distinguishes a true human being from lower life forms (like worms) is our ability to choose—the ability to exercise our freedom of choice (why can't I be a member of both Greenpeace and the N.R.A. if I want to?).

Unfortunately, in this modern society, we are not often allowed to make all the choices we wish we could make, and, sadly enough, those few times we do exercise our sacred right, we often seem to make the "wrong" choice. So, what can we do?

John Smith is a bank clerk in Smallville, California. He got married 23 years ago, no children, and now, he is just a few years away from retiring. He and his wife, Joanne, drive an old Ford and spend a lot of their free time in front of the TV. Often, they complain to each other. They feel threatened by the proliferation of gang warfare in nearby Los Angeles and by violent crime even closer to home. They are perplexed by massive government spending and sudden economic crises, saddened by homelessness and illiteracy, and overwhelmed by new technologies, by global warming, by the spread of killer bees, and by the relentless extinction of animals with which they used to share this planet. The beautiful bluebirds that Joanne loved to feed 20 years ago when they first bought their house now seem to have vanished— like many of her younger dreams. The Smiths and others like them sometimes think, "Even if I could get my life in order, what good would it do?"

Some people indeed feel powerless and insignificant when it comes to social issues and world events. We often think that, even if we do everything right and make the right choices, our welfare is still at the mercy of powerful others. This kind of belief system leads to a feeling of being out of control and impotent, unable to create change to any significant degree. "Why even try?" asks Mr. Smith.

Freedom

"Give me liberty or give me death," cried Patrick Henry.

The Constitution is supposed to safeguard and guarantee life, liberty, and the pursuit of happiness, since real choices can be made only in a free environment. A decision can be conscious or not, but to be defined as free, it has to be reached without external coercion or trickery. A small child to whom is given a poisoned candy is not choosing between life and death; he is not free to choose.

Freedom implies knowledge. If there is no conscious understanding of the various options, there can be no freedom of choice. Ignorance (or better still, dis-information) about our democratic system among citizens of the former Soviet Union distorted their value system and did not allow them to make a choice. Once the Berlin Wall crumbled, millions were able to "see" better and were better able to exercise their freedom of choice.

True choices are inseparable from true freedom and from real knowledge. What distinguishes human beings from animals is our greater ability to make choices, even if sometimes not always in "tune with" our biological instincts. Both man and animals are afraid of and escape from fire, but animals do not willingly start fires; man does. Animals are bound by their instincts and enjoy a limited amount of free choice concerning their self-identity and their perception of the world.

Human beings possess a considerably greater awareness of their self-identity, a greater ability to process information about their own experiences and the world that surrounds them, and, most important, they are able to make unpredictable, and sometimes, self-destructive decisions. This ability is possible only through the free association of neurons in the brain and the free environment within man's psyche (there was a song in the 70s, that stated: "Freedom is inside your head"). Without freedom of choice, human behavior is stifled, stagnant and repetitive. Without freedom to innovate, search, explore, and act, there is no growth, no fulfillment of man's inner drive, and no joy.

Following our binary matrix, we can distinguish between two kinds of freedom: 1. Individual freedom (for the one) and 2. Group freedom or liberty (for the many). Here, I define freedom as the individual's need to express himself or herself, including his or her choices. I define liberty as the freedom of the community or the need of the group to express its own self-identity, its desires, and its choices (culture, tradition, etc.).

In the area of government and politics, liberty is a concept, which has always given and continues to give inspiration and excitement. Liberty is a right and a privilege, but also a responsibility. It comes with the duty to preserve the freedom of others, and, by that, it is somewhat limited. A land of liberty is a land in which all subjects are restrained and considered in their actions by what can be harmful or detrimental to others. Government, in this respect, is chosen as the referee and judge who determines the limits of individual freedoms in terms of the benefit to the liberty of the society.

After hundreds of years of conflict, even today, our society seems to offer a limited choice between right and left, between two ideologies, both of which are rooted in self-interest. As discussed in the chapters about political economics, both the capitalistic system (based on Adam Smith's economic model) and the socialist system (based on Karl Marx's economic and social construct) have failed in the sense that they have placed the individual at the center of their study. It is necessary to drastically reverse the priorities of both systems in the fields of economics and social studies and place the welfare of the community as their main priority, with the interests of the individual taking on a secondary role. In other words, both capitalism and socialism are essentially self-centered ideologies, while other solutions, like the "third way", proposed, among others, by British Prime Minister Tony Blair, are nothing but a poor mixture of capitalist, socialist, and communist ideas.

A genuine alternative can be found only in a radical reversal of priorities, placing the good of the many first and paramount without denying the basic, absolute, inalienable rights of the individual: life, liberty, and the freedom necessary to pursue one's happiness. Economically speaking, this would translate into a balanced combination of free market principles with responsible social, community, and environmental programs.

END NOTES

Economic freedom

Managers and marketing specialists have always wondered whether the consumer really does have genuine freedom of choice or whether his opinions and desires can be entirely manipulated, hence, directed towards certain products instead of others. Our actions and choices are, in fact, mostly influenced by our daily needs and desires. We need to research whether these needs and desires originate from innate and unchanging elements or whether our psyche can actually be manipulated in such a way that we subconsciously adopt those desires that are suggested to us by the attractive images of ads and commercials, with their daily ratio of illusion and virtual reality. First and foremost, television is the medium that continuously bombards us with more or less hidden messages.

One of the main objectives of this theory of value is to discover what actually determines human desires and needs—those factors that, in turn, give rise to the value of goods, determine beliefs, and produce actions and behaviors. Finally, all this comes down to the question of how decisions are actually made, which brings us back to the question of freedom of choice and its role in modern society.

Throughout the past century, people everywhere, in both democratic and communist socio-cultural environments, have tended to indulge in a mode of thinking that can be described as essentially materialistic (though the methods and means have greatly varied). This frame of mind has served to justify a type of attitude and a set of business practices that can be best summed up as absolute pragmatism (a nice way of saying that the world of business is like shark-infested waters), with the quest for profit being the sole, non-negotiable objective. It is also true, on the other hand, that we are now experiencing a historical turning point in which mankind, as a whole, is desperately looking for new values and ideals; some are hoping to achieve a so-called new world order while others are hoping to get, at least, some order in their heads or in their checkbooks.

As the flags of greater freedom wave in a host of former communist nations, and while centralized economies are on the run and bureaucracies are being improved (well, almost everywhere, excluding most of Italy, lots of Motor Vehicle Departments, the Social Security Administration, Veterans Hospitals, etc. etc . . . . well, you get my point), the battle for global markets is going on at a faster rate than ever, and in more unscrupulous ways.

The drive to conquer markets has replaced the arms race, but there is a great danger in the serious lack of moral and ethical principles and in the absence of a common standard of values. The call, heard in the West, of "Capitalists of the world, unite!" and echoed by that heard in Southern California "Venture capitalists of the web, innovate!" should be tempered by rules and regulations aimed at protecting the interests of workers and consumers.

Milton Friedman, one of the top economists of the 20th century, in his paper on *The Basis of Value Judgments in Economics*, sees "another, and very different dimension in modern economics. The role of the market has changed in a device for the voluntary cooperation of many individuals in the establishment of common values."

For Friedman, in this new dimension of the economic life of society, "free exchange" and "free market" cover a far broader range than a narrowly economic one. Friedman applies the same analysis of the free market to free speech and freedom of activity. Freedom to sell and freedom to speak do not imply having a buyer or an audience. They only imply having the opportunity to seek one and having a mutually beneficial interaction with it. For Friedman, "The essence of free speech, as of free exchange, is the mutual benefit of the participants."

In this sense, Friedman would agree with my argument that genuine freedom is closely connected to the concept of the welfare of the whole, the benefit for the greatest number.

I believe that it is hard to dispute that the greatest freedoms (and freedom of choice, which includes strategic alternatives) are directly dependent on the welfare and well-being of the whole. In fact, when values, purposes, and activities reflect a concern and dedication to the benefit of the whole society, they reveal a higher degree of freedom. Conversely, when values and purposes exhibit a limited concern with a small number of individuals, or with a single one, the amplitude of free choices becomes severely limited.

Decision theory has amassed, in its short life, a large amount of literature and an even greater number of conflicting hypotheses. Sometimes known as DSS (Decision Support System), decision theory, today, is computer-driven and mostly mathematical in nature. While DSS can greatly help in logistic problems—the routings of planes or trailers, the mix of chemicals in a host of industries, the switching of telecommunication systems, etc.—it cannot be easily applied to systems that involve human choices and reactions. The reason can be found in the *erroneous assumption* (used and abused by utilitarianists and by most microeconomic theories) that it is possible to define a regular sequence in the variables (the preference function) to form definable curves. Economists have tried to use linear and non-linear programming as an elaborate tool for the reduction of complex qualitative problems into quantitative forms, such as the problem of what constitutes economic value, but have not been able to apply it other than in situations where human choice was limited or nonexistent.

The assumption that it is possible to weigh human choices, even if by an ordinal measure of utility [14], should be re-evaluated, and a new paradigm should be found that can accommodate freedom of choice and the human sense of responsibility towards the whole (even when choices are not in the best interests of the individual, such as: a soldier sacrificing his life for his country, a fireman risking his life for another human being, or a medical doctor risking his or her life to help cure others, etc.).

It would be cumbersome to cover the many philosophical, social, and economic concepts associated with the question of choice, but it is necessary to touch on the question of determinism.

Determinism and indeterminism play an important role in the understanding of human life. Virtually no major philosopher has claimed that everything that happens is inevitable. And, yet, it is not easy to find the line of demarcation between the world of historical inevitability and the realm of man's free will and action.

Augustine, Bishop of Hippo (about 400 years after Jesus Christ), was one of the first great Christian thinkers who tried to find the relationship between freedom and necessity. His vision of a constant presence of sin in man's history did not contradict his desire for freedom. For Augustine, man is free as long as he does what is just and right, but, when man does evil, he becomes "free of justice and slave of sin." Unfortunately, St. Augustine did not stop there. He tried to combine man's free will with a supernatural "Grace" given from above. The conclusion was that mankind must cooperate with the Divine Grace in order to reach salvation. This mixture of philosophical and theological approaches complicated Augustine's view of the human condition and of what constitutes free will and free choice.

Centuries later, Christianity secularized Augustine's conception of the struggle between the "Civitas Dei" (The City of God) and the "Civitas Terrena" (the Earthly City), interpreting history, from the fall of Adam and Eve to the resurrection of Jesus Christ, not as unique historical events but only as symbols of the fall of all men from good and of man's restoration to good. It is for this very reason that the Catholic Church lost, particularly through the Middle Ages, the human element of freedom and freedom of choice.

Martin Luther (1483-1546) and his partial "return" to Augustinian positions (stressing the individual's freedom of choice and one's ability to establish his or her personal relationship with the Divinity) led to the Protestant emphasis on the ability of men to choose. The Protestant work ethic and the drive to achieve earthly success (often translated into monetary terms) were derived from Luther, Calvin, and other early Protestant philosophers.

However, it is only through the convoluted explanations of Max Weber that Calvin's belief in absolute predestination could be linked to taking one's destiny into one's own hands. In some ways, the Catholic view, with its emphasis on good works, leaves more room for human freedom than Calvin's notion of predetermined grace.

It is interesting to note that most Western philosophers are influenced by their Judeo-Christian tradition, and that most of the literature dealing with the process of "free will" emphasizes man's will and intellect rather than man's actions and feelings. (A little too much "Mars" and too little "Venus." What!? You did not read that bestseller, *Men are from Mars, Women are from Venus*?)

So, today, following the definitions outlined in previous pages, it seems necessary to try to re-interpret human behavior (desires and choices) by placing more significance on man's emotions (particularly love) and heart, and a little less on man's will and intellect. By doing so, we can approach the problem of human free will and historical determinism in a unique way.

But what kind of process produces choices? What are the leading values by which choices are, or should be, made? For some philosophers (Plato), political considerations should be on top of the list. For others (Marx), the determining factors in the shaping of history, and, therefore, of human life, are to be found in the economic realm (the struggle between the production forces and the production relations). For still others, such as Arnold Toynbee, religious and spiritual relationships form the core element in determining success and failure, both in human lives and in history as a whole, including economic history.

Returning to Milton Friedman: "The whole wondrous body of modern scientific knowledge has been built up by free exchange in the market place for ideas." Other economists and philosophers also share Friedman's idea that freedom of choice is mainly responsible for the advances in academic pursuit, the development of language, the structure of common law, and other "structures capable of gradual evolution. It seems that evolution and progress can come about more easily through the voluntary cooperation of free individuals." Friedman continues by asking:

What is a desirable mechanism for the preservation
of such a set of values (an 'integrative' system, a common

set of values), which yet retains the possibility for change. Here is where I suggest that economic analysis can contribute most to the political scientist and the philosopher. In many ways, this is the basic role of the free market in both goods and ideas to enable mankind to cooperate in this process of searching for and developing values.

The mechanism needed for the development of an integrative system of values can be found in a system of thought that allows both determinism (based on unchanging values determined by the unchanging purpose of man's existence: his and her self-fulfillment) and indeterminism (based on changing values determined by man's freedom).

To develop this system of thought, we need to distinguish between those elements that are common to all human beings and those factors that are unique to each individual. Just as purpose can be divided into two basic types (individual and holistic), human choices can fall into one of the two categories: choices made by the community and choices made by one individual alone. When dealing with the individual, it is almost impossible to predetermine his or her choice, since the parameters of individual freedom remain, mainly, inside the individual's mind and heart. When dealing with a group, on the other hand, it is much easier to ascertain (sometimes even calculate) the type of reaction and the choices the group will make in response to a certain situation.

Arranging different types of choices in hierarchical order and matching them to the binary set described before, it is possible to make a diagram.

A) INDIVIDUAL CHOICES
   OF AN INTERNAL/INTANGIBLE NATURE:
   Very high level of freedom of choice.
B) COLLECTIVE CHOICES
   OF AN INTERNAL/INTANGIBLE NATURE:
   Medium / high level of freedom of choice.

C) INDIVIDUAL CHOICES
   OF A MATERIAL NATURE:
   Medium / low level of freedom of choice.
D) COLLECTIVE CHOICES
   OF A MATERIAL NATURE:
   Very low level of freedom of choice.

In fact, when we reach the deepest roots of human behavior, we find that, whenever a biological imperative dictates choices, freedom is almost entirely lost, subjected to our physiological needs and urges. Here, freedom seems to give way to the *Laws of Nature*. But, when we enter the realm of the mind and heart, then our choices multiply and freedom grows and prospers.

I do not want to give the impression that there are two parallel realities, i.e., nature/no-freedom and mind/freedom, and that the two never meet. The inner world of the mind and the outer world of the body may look separate, but they are, in fact, inexorably connected (at least as far as human beings are concerned). We perceive them as separate realms because of our inborn forma-mentis. From the primary concept of "one (inner self)—many (outer world)," we categorize reality following the binary matrix.

This conclusion may also lead to an important inference: the difference between determinism (fatalism) and indeterminism (free choice) should center on the issue of human responsibility. If this inference is possible, then we should find that a combination of determinism and indeterminism could better explain the human situation. The problem in the past has been the focus of the argument.

In asking if we are free or not, we should shift the focus of the question to *whether or not we are willing and able to exercise our ability to choose (are we responsible or not).*

The focus should be on human responsibility. Our ability to respond to the stimuli and challenges that confront us everyday, our interpretation of what those challenges and stimuli mean, and our ability to collect relevant and true data relative to our choices should be the center of our decision-making process. The distinction between determinism and indeterminism should be centered on the human element of responsibility. This distinction between being able or unable to respond to challenges should have precedence over and above a distinction based on the moral elements of good (what a certain culture defines as good) and evil (what is defined as bad by a group of people). The obvious implication of this conditional definition, however we take it, is that human values should be considered, in their development, as both conditional and unconditional, contingent and necessary, probabilistic and deterministic.

Our individual and collective value systems and our understanding of their importance in our life guide us in making choices. Thus, we can say that these choices arise from a combination of predetermined elements, such as the cultural principles of a family or social group, and variable elements, such as creativity, personal response ability, and the specific characteristics of an individual. In other words, this means that human choices can only be dictated and manipulated up to a certain point, beyond which this external influence will clash with our human individuality, i.e., with that basic quality that makes each human being unique—his or her particular purpose in life.

In fact, as we go down toward the most basic, material, and physiological needs of human beings, we find freedom almost completely overpowered by necessity. At this lowest point, when biological forces dictate choices, freedom seems to vanish, giving room to the tyranny of natural laws.

Material values, particularly those associated with man's most fundamental needs (food, air, clothing, shelter, health), can be clearly predicted. Other less essential material values (fashionable clothes, house appliances, means of transportation, etc.) can be forecast with a relatively high degree of accuracy. Communal values of a spiritual nature (common values, such as love, liberty, life, and the free pursuit of happiness) can be organized and forecast with a moderate to high degree of accuracy. But, even the value of one's life is not universal and can vary (just look at the suicide bombers of today's Palestine). Only individual values of a conceptual nature have such a high level of freedom, since they are related to man's virtually unlimited degree of creativity, that they cannot easily be forecasted or predicted.

Values and perceptions of values produce choices. Therefore, choices are a combination of predetermined factors, such as the cultural values installed in the individual's mind and heart by his society (family, community, religion, etc.), as well as undetermined factors, such as the individual's own creativity, his "response ability," and personal characteristics. At the opposite pole, we find Karl Marx's value theory.

The whole communist system rests on Marx's economic theories: economic value theory, dialectic and class struggle, and historical materialism; and even Fidel Castro would agree that, of these three pillars, Marx's theory of economic value is the central mast. According to Marx, economic value is determined by labor, that is, by the amount of hours of labor placed in the production of goods. Today, we know very well that, even if some poor soul worked hundreds of hours to make an unusable or unwanted machine (say a car with square wheels), the value of that product would be zero. Marx's idea that value was the product of labor (particularly manual labor) was necessary in order to create a sense of guilt in the ruling class (they should have, if you look at the conditions in which some miners worked and lived) in order to instill a sense of righteous anger in the so-called working class and in order to justify a violent revolution.

The extensive references to other philosophers and the convoluted explanations helped convince many intellectuals then, and even today, of the validity of his arguments. Marx's observation about the squalid conditions of the working poor of his day (like in many third world countries today) might have been correct, but his conclusions and his theories made absolutely no economic sense whatsoever. The economic value of a thing (surplus value, as he called it, value-added we call it today) does not derive from labor but comes from the desire (demand) of the market for that thing. What today may have a lot of added-on value, like a new

Pentium IV processor, a new restaurant, or a fashionable label, tomorrow's demand may change and bring its value to a fraction of today. Economics should not be ruled by anger or guilt but rather by a clear understanding of the fraternal and inter-related nature of men and women. Real values cannot be distorted or hidden for long. Human ability to understand and to choose cannot be repressed.

In other words, choices and values can be manipulated only to a point. Beyond that point rests human individuality and those characteristics that make man what he is. It is his unique purpose for existence.

The essence of human purpose cannot be changed, just like the purpose of the human lungs or brain cannot be modified without destroying the whole organism. It follows that certain human values (beauty, truth, love, justice, freedom, and other ideals), those stemming from the very essential, inner nature of man, cannot be changed by cultures or modified by history. These are the common values that should form the foundation of a globally acceptable value system and a globally acceptable economy, and the search for these common values and principles should be at the forefront of any innovative value theory.

CHAPTER IV

STRATEGIC PLANNING

Learning Strategy

S cience fiction seems to be everywhere, from cartoons to decade-running mega-epics, like *Star Wars,* or endless TV series, like *Star Trek.* Personally, I like the way fantasy extrapolates possible futures from bits and pieces of scientific facts.

One of the great masters of sci-fi was the late Isaac Asimov, and his greatest work, the *Foundation* epic, has been a landmark in sci-fi literature.

The Foundation stories are set in a distant future, when humans have mastered travel through hyperspace, and the human race is spread over most of the galaxy. But, even a thousand years into the future, human emotions and character remain what they are today, with all our problems and weaknesses. In Asimov's story, the Galactic Empire seems to be destined for centuries of prosperity. But one scientist, Harry Seldon, while laying the foundations for the new scientific study of psychohistory, sees signs of danger. With the use of complicated mathematical formulas, Harry and his assistants learn to predict, with some approximation, future trends and events. In so doing, they discover that human civilization is on the brink of a long and dark age.

From before the time the Pyramids were built until today, many people have tried to predict upcoming trends and events, including shrewd political analysts, media and advertising gurus, fashion connoisseurs, and raving hordes of economic and financial advisers (please beware!).

The truth is that, so far, nobody can read the future. It is equally true that there are some tools, statistical and other, that can be used to assess the present and predict some possible futures. (If you want to study possible futures, check the World Future Society, one of the most respected and solid organization in the field. And, yes, of course, I am a long time professional member of this international institution.)

Strategic planning and performance management are just a few of the many tools used in predicting and preparing for future scenarios. The next pages deal with some of these techniques, but from a unique perspective—that of the binary matrix.

RELATIONAL ANALYSIS

First: Analyze

I often traveled and worked in Japan, doing consulting work for Japanese companies. And one recurring observation I received from Japanese businessmen was that "Americans are too critical and analytical."

To a certain extent, that is true. But even though Western culture and civilization has been criticized for being too analytical and for too often displaying a desire to strip and search the most minute details of a sometimes complicated problem, it is only through a careful and correct analysis that we can truly understand the essential elements of a problem or a situation. Only after that can we try to reconstruct and rebuild a new system and a new sum of solutions.

Therefore, analysis is the critical starting point for strategic thinking, though *not* its final objective, and the executive who wants to familiarize himself or herself with strategic planning, needs, at first, to be a good analyst.

Peter Drucker, one of the early gurus of modern management, wrote, "The right questions can be asked, and answered, only after [we do] an analysis of the activities necessary to attain specific objectives."

The strategic thinker, when faced with problems, situations, events, or trends that appear on the scene as a monolith, must first dissect them into their most elemental parts. In this way, having understood the meaning of these essential elements, the strategist can more easily rebuild a new "set" and find solutions where before there were problems.

Connected to analysis is vision.

A four-star general told me, "Even if you got good weapons but you do not have trained people behind the weapons, the weapons are useless. If you got both, but have no good strategy, weapons and people will not win. First, you must have the right strategy to accomplish the purpose and implement the vision."

The right strategy and a feasible vision are two other keys in implementing a successful plan.

Another essential characteristic of strategic planning is intellectual elasticity. After deep analysis of a problem or a situation, the corporate executive (assuming he or she is doing the planning) needs a substantial dose of intellectual flexibility in order to arrive at realistic solutions to the problems being analyzed (no Talibans allowed here).

It is not enough to simply dissect with great precision and paint elegant business plans with different shades of color. It is important to be able to find innovative solutions to an ever-changing set of circumstances.

Phenomena and events in our society often do not fit in a linear model, therefore, the step-by-step methodology, such as systems analysis, may not always be the most useful in analyzing and re-assembling a particular situation. Rather, it is the non-linear, "circular," or, better still, "spherical" type of thinking (after all, we live in a three-dimensional world) that is most likely to bring about a solution to a complicated challenge. (Remember the interstellar chase in the movie *Star Trek: The Wrath of Kan*? "Think three-dimensional".)

What modern strategic climbers need is a thorough understanding of what constitutes a problem and a complete understanding of how all aspects of this world affect or depend on one another. In other words, it is necessary to be flexible, understanding the ***relational nature of our perceptions*** (and the binary matrix), and adopt a relational mode of thought and analysis (note that the binary matrix has three dimensions: "one-many" constitute the horizontal plane, "in-out" gives it depth).

An example of binary analysis can be made in the listing of a company's assets. When preparing a strategic plan or even the annual financial statement, the wise executive lists both tangible and intangible assets. We all know what the tangible assets are, but often we do not value enough intangible gems, such as intellectual capital (in-house expertise, R&D, patents, specialized sales force), unique relationships (with customers, government, and vendors), special processes and favorable financing, brand equity (reputation, recognition), and other valuable, less tangible assets.

In adding value to a product or service (and to a balance sheet), we need to consider the two dimensions of tangible, material assets, as well as the intangible, less visible ones.

Speaking of value-added, let's remember that brand equity (the company's good name, reputation and trust) is becoming an ever more important part of a firm's genuine assets (I wish it was the same with politicians).

Another important asset in any organization is the quality of its people and, particularly, of its leaders (just read any book on military strategy and tactics). And, among all the skills of top management, one of the most valuable is (without question) the ability of the leaders to adapt to changing circumstances, to face up and overcome challenges and crises (like New York's former mayor Rudy Giuliani).

Strength of character (lucidity under stress), great mental flexibility, and adaptable approaches are the essential traits of good leadership (ask any soldier).

Also, in nature, a gene pool that is totally lacking in flexibility and variation will be unable to adapt to changing circumstances (ask any biologist). With a changing environment, genetically encoded knowledge needs to adapt, or it becomes a burden, with consequences that can be fatal to that species' survival.

A similar process operates within us as individuals. We all have a rich repertoire of ideas and concepts, based on past experiences, which enable us to survive (be nice to your mother-in-law or to that policeman who just stopped you for speeding) and prosper (be nice to your boss). Without any provision for variation and improvement, our habitual ideas become dull and lose their advantages and, in the end, we are defeated in our competition with our rivals or by a fast-changing environment.

NATURE'S STRATEGY
TWO RULES: SEX AND SURVIVAL

Or survival and sex, as you wish

Two forces, two instincts rule our lives: survival and sex. And, if economic survival can make you lose sleep (unless you are an Enron Executive), sex can get you in real trouble . . . as it always did, since the time of the Garden of Eden.

Some people say that we are what we eat. I say *we are what we do*. And, to us, we are the way we perceive ourselves and our actions.

If you strongly believe in the selfish nature of men, and I do not dispute the fact that most of us are utterly selfish in nature, just consider the greatest instinct of any living form: *survival* (not necessarily the TV rendering of desert island castaways).

Rule Number One: *SURVIVAL*

When dissecting this primordial force (very familiar to the founders of Netscape and other new-economy entrepreneurs), we notice that, in order to survive, one must first be able to nurture and maintain one's body. In the case of a business, survival means to be able to maintain (or better still, improve) the company's financial position.

In human terms, it can be more effectively accomplished if your mind is sharp and you are emotionally stable (boot camp's motto: Adapt and overcome); in business, it means to have management with brains.

So, to survive means to satisfy our bodily needs (remember the screaming babies in the maternity ward?), and to allow our mind to work properly so our body can do what it needs to do to stay alive. *Mens sana in corpore sano* used to be the ancient Romans' favorite motto (which translates to "a healthy mind in a healthy body").

Surviving does not simply mean getting by. We want to have a good life and a long life . . . a very long one, if possible. I know I do.

As I write these pages on my laptop, while listening to "The Long and Winding Road", one of the Beatles' top songs from the *White Album*, it seems just a few days ago that I was spear fishing, over thirty years ago, along the Italian beaches, just outside of Circeo, about a hundred miles south of Rome. I know I want to live and survive much longer, and so do you!

Some people (my age and older) boast that they had a long and productive life. So did I. But I would be willing to go on a lot longer . . . if given the chance.

So, let's be honest. Our truer instinct, our deeper desire is for our life to go on and on and on. So, what can we do about it? Nature has a way to help us . . . by proxy. After having taken care of one's immediate survival needs, we notice that all living creatures possess (or become possessed by) another overpowering primordial force: *reproduction*, or to put it in human terms, "*sex.*"

Rule Number Two: *SEX*
(or the quest for the future)

Reproduction can be viewed as a form of survival. Of course, if we could choose between passing on our genes through our progeny (the spoiled brats) or overcoming old age and death, I doubt anyone would think twice about staying "here." But, not having that choice, we go along with nature's way to ensure the passing on of at least some of our genes (not necessarily always the best ones!).

Our desire for survival expresses itself in various forms. First, there is survival in the biological sense, of living on in our children. But, there is also a metaphysical survival that indicates life after death (be it reincarnation, or the migration of souls, life in a spiritual world, or the resurrection of one's essence in a future time).

Human beings express this desire to live on, to a certain degree, also by leaving behind lasting symbols of their presence (statues, monuments, music and other works of art, scholarly and scientific legacies, endowments, etc.).

But it is sexual reproduction that takes most of our energies. *Immortality, in this sense, means the ability of a species to exist beyond the deaths of its individual members.*

Multiplication of one's own "self" starts early on, when sperm meets egg, and our first cell starts to divide and divide and divide (and so do bacteria and plants and flowers and fish and cats and dogs and so on).

From reproducing copies of their DNA at the cellular level, organisms quickly graduate to a higher level: reproducing not only exact copies, but even improved replicas of themselves (imagine the possibilities if Microsoft is forced to split).

Life needs reproduction. Survival alone, without reproduction, leads to a dead end, literally.

Maybe that's why Mother Nature has made reproduction such an enjoyable activity. It wanted to make sure that nobody forgot about it, so it made certain we had so much fun doing it (I hope you do . . . too).

Reproduction breeds a new primordial force—that of *caring for one's own offspring*. This is a really powerful force, particularly among more evolved forms of life. Try getting too close to the cubs of a grizzly bear and see what maternal instinct can do to you. Caring for the new generation is the hallmark of most advanced species (that's why men and women who abandon their children are no better than worms).

Let me add that taking steps to reduce the ozone layer, preserving the biosphere by eliminating harmful pollution, protecting endangered species, and so on, are also ways of caring for our future offspring (not just trust funds and passbook savings for our spoiled brats' outlandish college tuitions) and should not be the sole province of eco-freaks, but the genuine concern of forward-looking economists and industry leaders as well.

From parental instincts emerge *collective behaviors*. Collective behaviors resemble parental instincts in the sense that communities of organisms, from fish to insects (at least those species who possess strong communal ties), behave primarily out of concern for the well-being of the community and the community's offspring (bees, ants).

In this way, we notice that the creation of complex organisms witnesses the remarkable strategy of organizing, self-maintaining, community-support systems. These DNA-encoded systems (the Genetic Matrix) improve considerably the chances of continuity and expansion of the genetic pool. This type of survival of the species is done through the passing on of vital information.

Somehow, there seems to be a turning point (particularly in organisms with a more developed parental and collective instinct) when the "sense" of community (indeed the *value* of the community) overshadows even the survival instinct of the individual.

Taken by itself, the individual ant, bee, fish or red-blood cell, may still have as its core value its own survival, but when confronted with harm to the whole community (be it the ants' hill, the bee hive, or our own bodies), the survival of the group (what I call Collective Response Mechanisms) becomes the dominant force, even at the cost of the life of the individual.

That's why we love heroes. From real-life people, like George Washington or Abraham Lincoln, to less-real ones like Hercules or Xena, we love people with a strong sense of dedication, those who care for and protect our communities (our society's T-cells).

Caring for the next generation, for the community, and for one's turf is also part of both rules (survival and sex). Thus, we return to the "one-many" matrix.

Even in survival, human beings display a binary set of complementary and interwoven instincts: first, the preservation of the self (the one) and second, the reproduction, multiplication, and preservation of one's progeny, community and environment (the many). The two instincts complement each other to the point of blending into one single, swirling energy.

The minute differences in the mix of these forces define the infinite variety of behaviors of living creatures. It is this endless spectrum of possibilities that makes nature so beautifully varied and awesome.

Here, someone may perceive what appears to be faulty logic. Though I emphasize the double aspect of care for self/others, it may seem that first, there is the care for the self, and, then, through multiplication, the care for others emerges out of nothing (or rather, out of the circumstances). That is not correct. The key is paying attention to how real people behave, analyzing all aspects of human nature. The point is this: dealing with others reveals an aspect of our nature that is other than the concern for self-preservation, but survival does not create it. Collective behavior was always there, somehow, right from the beginning, etched in our (and all living beings') genes.

At this point, two important footnotes are due. First, in the instinctual force of preserving one's own self and community, *a strong tendency is also evident in all living beings to preserve and protect their territory and environment* (this includes personal, business, and socio-political turfs). If you know some politician, you know how they can be as defensive about their territory as a grizzly bear. Second, We have not yet begun to unravel the message hidden in our DNA. I go absolutely nuts when I hear supposedly knowledgeable scientists saying that a lot of the human DNA is "junk" and that lots of "information" has little or no effect on the making of a human being.

Nature is very efficient and does not waste energy or resources on needless projects. A mosquito has a lot of eyes, are they too many? No. A centipede has a lot of legs, are they wasted? No. Are there too many leaves on an oak tree? Are there too many suction cups on an octopus' tentacles? So, believe me, if humans have been passing along that much information in our DNA, there is a reason. Ok, as far as we know now, we are not using much of that information for our bodily functions, but maybe we will in future generations!!! I don't know what those extra DNA instructions are for, but if you asked me if I wanted to be born with a full set of DNA or without what those biologists say we are not using, I say give it all to me. And, believe me, those so-called scientists would like to have it all too.

THE GAIA PRINCIPLE

A Living Planet?

Do you love white, sandy beaches? Maybe we like tropical islands because we sense the multitude of life bursting, just under the waves, in the coral reefs. Or, maybe we love those calm, clear, warm, shallow seas because it is there that our DNA resonates louder, in tune with its watery origins. Let's face it, we love nature.

We know we are connected with all life on this planet. But, to what extent? Can't we pollute the planet, just a little?

Ecology and economy can go hand in hand.

Proposed by British scientist James Lovelock about 30 years ago, the Gaia Theory has evolved, in one form or another, finding increasing acceptance among environmentalists and natural scientists.

In the early 1960s, NASA asked Lovelock to be part of a study in the search for life on Mars. From this original study arose the idea of separating planets that were considered "dead," like Mercury, from living ones, like Earth. In 1969, Lovelock first presented, at a scientific conference on the origin of life, his theory of a "comprehensive definition of life." The Gaia theory is named after the Greek goddess of the earth. This theory has found supporters as well as critics. Among the supporters, two types of interpretation of the Gaia principle tend to emerge.

The Gaia principle proposes that all living organisms, as well as the physical environment in which they live and interact, exist as one united being. This hypothesis has been described as more complex than ancient naturalism. The Gaia principle views the earth and all its living beings, including mankind, as one vast organism. According to Lovelock: *"Life and its environment can be considered as a single entity, which tries to regulate physical conditions in order to keep the environment at a comfortable state for the organisms themselves."*

Other less animistic interpreters of the Gaia principle believe that it is teamwork, between the different living organisms and the environment in which they exist, that somehow is responsible for the conditions created in order to support themselves, as well as other, diverse types of life.

On one side, there are scientists, some of whom study the earth's physical and chemical cycles (earth systems scientists), who are intrigued by the global feedback loops and the intricate cycles that keep oxygen levels and global temperature from fluctuating to extremes. The other group of supporters is sometimes dismissed as "eco-freaks" because of their stress on the consciousness attributed to the planet or to nature itself.

A great article in *Natural History* (June 2001) by Lynn Margulis and D. Sagan exemplify the inter-connectivity of all living beings. Recent discoveries in the hot (temperatures may exceed 500 degrees), deep-sea vents where ancient microbes, named Archea, have been found, have raised the possibility that life may exist elsewhere beyond our planet. By the way, these so-called microbes (that can live also without oxygen, digesting iron or sulfur) have been found (alive) also in freezing, 1,000-feet deep rocks.

While it is within the realm of science to assume a purposeful order in any system, it is a big step to imply consciousness from mere purpose. In other words, a well-oiled machine or a good software program may have an inner purpose, but this does not imply self-consciousness.

In the case of non-living systems (like machines, computer software, and most governmental agencies), *purpose is generally generated outside of the object* (by Mr. Henry Ford, by Mr. Bill Gates, or by some convoluted Congressional Committee).

A painting, a statue, or a machine (a car or computer), for example, derives its shape, mechanism, and function from the purpose given to it by its creator. In the case of living beings, it seems that the purpose of their behavior and function is either given to them by some external being (if you are a believer), or it can be considered as genetically inborn (if you are more scientifically minded), and then passed on, from generation to generation, through the genetic code (the data depository and its coded key). In either case, it seems a little extreme to infer a collective consciousness encompassing both living organisms and lifeless matter.

The reason this theory is important to the economic value theory is that, for the last two centuries, economists have been regarding the economic environment as a sort of Darwinian jungle and, based on these assumptions, have tried to build a system of economic "laws."

Evolutionists, like many economists, see the world as a battlefield where living organisms battle for supremacy in a fight for the survival of the fittest. But today, genetic biologists have recognized the absolute interdependence of all living organisms and their environments.

Almost three centuries ago, the German philosopher, Gottfried Leibniz (1646-1716), a child prodigy who wrote his first treatise at the age of twenty (in which he anticipated later discoveries in logic and mathematics), had proposed a new approach to reality. According to Leibniz, the universe is made of many individual elements (he called them Monads) that exist by themselves ("windowless"). But, the Monads interact with each other, making all the attributes of this "substance" necessarily connected. For Leibniz, what is real is constituted by interconnected beings, whatever one Monad does, the whole perceives; whatever happens to the whole, each monad feels (I wonder if Leibniz studied Buddhism).

Studies by microbiologists, such as Lynn Margulis, Professor at the University of Massachusetts, Kwang Jeon from the University of Tennessee, and Tyler Volk from New York University, have proven that simple, elementary organisms, such as amoebas and bacteria, can actually be induced to create a symbiotic relationship. In this symbiotic world, living systems become embedded in other living organisms. According to microbiologist Gail Fleischaker, "What survives as a symbiotic relationship is, of necessity, cooperative organisms rather than purely competitive ones."

Evolution and development began with the impulse that exists in all living organisms to fulfill their full potential and accomplish the reason for their existence. In this sense, basic needs and desires, as well as individual and communal purposes, exist even prior to conception.

If you ever wondered what comes first, the chicken or the egg, the answer is clear: first came the data, the code, and then the genetic code.

The genetic material, imprinted in each organism, contains

not only the norms of behavior (the needs and desires necessary for the fulfillment of the individual, that for the survival and reproduction of the individual), it also contains data, material, and elements taken from the environment of which the genetic material is part.

In this way, the genetic code contains information that will support the individual in its quest for survival, its search for maturity, fulfillment, and reproduction, and its cooperation with (and dependence on) its environment.

The code also contains all elements necessary to connect the individual organism with the other communities of which it is going to be part (the proverbial flowers and bees).

Unfortunately, the business community has not taken the environmental cause seriously enough.

I favor a simple conclusion: We live on a planet that is clearly an interconnected and interdependent ecosystem, and, in making choices, we should consider their consequences.

I wish I could take you on a rowboat ride along the Po River in Italy, or on a gondola (those long, black, funny-shaped boats) in Venice's Canal Grande. Come for a swim in the Volga River in Russia on an early summer afternoon. It might not be as romantic as you would think. All these waters are brown and gray. There are chemicals dissolved in the water or floating on it that most chemists could not even name. The fish—the few still alive—are full of mercury and other poisons (other fish are beginning to look like those three-eyed, five-legged frogs found, in recent years, in Minnesota).

In the Ukraine, the radiation from nuclear plants (those that melted down a few years back, and those that did not . . . yet) seep into the rivers and into the water supplies. At night, the glow on most Eastern European rivers can be somewhat romantic . . . if you like fluorescent green as a color.

In an article titled "A Planet in Jeopardy," in *The Futurist* magazine, Lester R. Brown (President of the World Watch Institute) criticizes economists for being insensitive to the problem. Most economic planners consider even the most apparent problems, such as a host of diseases, pollution, and overpopulation crises, as but minor challenges. According to Brown, many economists "call for marginal course corrections as they pursue business as usual, but they lack an understanding of the carrying capacity of the ecological system."

Brown argues that economics and ecology are disciplines with intellectual frameworks that contrast starkly; consequently, they produce different views of the world we live in. The advances in technology and the use of alternative resources should seriously limit the archaic assumption that all economic resources are scarce or limited. Human resources should not be considered scarce, since it is self-evident that, with the proper training and with a social environment conducive to creativity and innovation, men and women are capable of unlimited wonders (just look at the computer skills and savvy in some God-forsaken parts of India).

Strategic studies have demonstrated that *the most effective way to find the ideal fit between an organization and its environment (its market and its customers) is to listen to the market, to learn from the environment, and to be responsive to the needs of the customers.*

In ecological terms, this means that economists and business executives should not consider ecological problems as non-essential and peripheral concerns but rather as an intrinsic part of the economic challenge. Today, we cannot ignore our dependence on a stable, natural environment, nor can we disregard the natural resources from which all economic goods are eventually derived.

ORGANIZATIONAL PLANNING

How to get organized

Once, somebody asked me about the difference between Heaven and Hell. They told me that in Heaven, all the great cooks are French, polite policemen are British, skillful mechanics are German, talented artists (and lovers) are Italian, and the sharp organization's committee is Swiss. In Hell, the cooks are British, the mechanics are French, the policemen are German, the artists are Swiss (there are no lovers in Hell), and of course the whole damn thing is badly run by the Italians. Considering the fact that I was born in Geneva, Switzerland, have lived for over 30 years in the good old U.S.A., and that my folks came from Italy, I may have something interesting to say (even if not well structured) about organizing principles.

Often, strategic planning is also referred to as organizational planning. Two of the main objectives of strategic and organizational planning are: 1. To identify the organizational plan, purpose, mission, goals, objectives, and programs of the organization, and 2. To understand the leadership role of the planner and the role of strategic management.

But first of all, what is an "organization"? And next, what is "strategy"?

Simply put, an organization is a system. And, what is a system? A system is a whole made up of different parts.

So, *an organization is an orderly system (an organized whole) composed of different parts with identifiable or orderly relationships among its elements, its parts or its members.*

The term organization has its root in the word *organism, a self-sustaining entity with a built-in purpose.* If we are talking about a business, the organization consists of the orderly relationship among its departments and the purpose (including self-preservation) given to it by the founders. If we're talking about a manufacturing plant, that organization is based on the orderly relationship of its different processes.

Sometimes the economy seems to be a chaotic system, like in Paul Ormerod's (the British economist) latest book: *Butterfly Economics*. In *Butterfly Economics*, Ormerod expands on the main point of his earlier book, *The Death of Economics*, namely that his fellow economists must drop classic economic determinism and accept the economic reality as chaotic, non-mechanistic and unpredictable. Some of the latest chaos theories, and the theory of fractals, seem to indicate that the swirls of air from the wings of a butterfly could, days later, trigger a hurricane. There is, of course, a sense in which some human events may have had a "butterfly" effect, triggering other closely related events. It comes to mind the American Revolution and the way it triggered the French Revolution and all the changes that remodeled the political landscape of Europe. Or Martin Luther's posting his ninety-five theses on the door of his church, and the radical changes that followed in most of fifteenth century Europe.

But we should also remember that these changes, like the butterfly's hurricane, couldn't take place unless there are some pre-existing conditions that allow the "domino effect."

Like the weather, economic activity may seem chaotic only because we have not yet identified its primary components and the way its forces interact (like winds, temperatures and pressure in the atmosphere; needs, desires and productive agents in human society). But life is not chaotic, it is rather well organized and with a clear sense of purpose.

When we observe that all living beings present a striving for survival and self-preservation, multiplication and cooperation, we notice that all life forms try to extend their existence beyond their individual life spans by organizing themselves into single entities with common goals and accepted rules of behavior. The same principle applies to other orderly systems (including business).

An important note is that, what has been preserved, however, is not the life of the individuals, but *the specialized information* that made possible the creation and thriving of that group of individuals. The essence of life, the DNA, is (more than anything else) a string of data, a code designed to interact with its environment. So, life strives for immortality, and, in a manner analogous to biological species, large organizations and institutions—such as the Roman Catholic Church, the Internal Revenue Service, Citicorp, or the United States Congress—also (in their unique ways) struggle for immortality.

When we deal with systems and with wholes and parts, we're talking about elementary concepts. What are these concepts? These concepts are (again) the concept of one and the concept of many.

When we're talking about a system, we are talking about a whole. Imagine a balloon or a sphere with a whole bunch of little balls or rocks inside. The big ball or sphere that contains the smaller rocks is the whole, while the little rocks or balls inside it are its parts or elements. So, a system is a whole made out of elements. The entire group is considered as one entity and the multitude of its individual components as its parts.

A systemic approach to business is a holistic approach, taking care of the internal as well as the external, the inside and the outside, the company and the customers, the business and its market environment.

The next thing to notice is that there are, essentially, two kinds of systems. The first system is an orderly or organized system. The second one is a chaotic, disorganized system.

An organized system is a system where the relationship between its parts is identifiable. A chaotic system is a system where the relationships among the different parts have no apparent or orderly relationship.

The weather, for example, can be considered a chaotic system. Because of its innumerable elements, which seem to move and interact randomly, it is almost impossible to predict the weather with precision and over lengthy periods of time. A house full of screaming babies can also be viewed as a chaotic system.

In orderly systems, like the circulatory system in the human body, for example, where our blood flows with rhythmic and predictable motion, there is a certain order. Inside the human body, there are orderly relationships among all its parts. Our digestive system is also an orderly system (as long as you do not eat hot chili peppers in a Mexican bodega, Polish sausage in Russia, or Italian pizza in Japan).

Our respiratory system is an orderly system (if you do not smoke more than two packs a day). The atoms inside a crystal form an orderly system (no doubt, unless you blow it to smithereens in an atomic blast). Hopefully, your organization is an orderly system. How about your life? Okay, let's not go there.

In math (if you remember that boring subject hardly studied

in high school), an organized system can also be defined as a function with two or more variables. One function might be the relation (f) between the whole (Y) and all its different elements (x1, x2, x3, x4, etc.). $Y = f(x)$.

The function, in an orderly system, is what rules or regulates the system. Y is "the one," x is "the many," and f is the various types of relationships they may have with each other.

In other words, in an organized system, there are some rules. Big deal! We know that. That's what defines the type of order we see: the rules.

In any organized system, there are some principles (the code, the operating system) that regulate that system (organization or organism). That's what makes it work in an orderly way. These are the functions, the conventions that regulate the relationship among the different elements, the laws and traditions that define a culture or a society.

The rules, that's what maintains the order. Like those huge volumes of corporate law books that fill the libraries of big (and expensive) law firms, every cell stores volumes of rules regarding its relationship with other cells in the organism (and how to deal with foreign intruders, too). Every time a cell divides, the codes get duplicated and passed on to the next generation. When the copying fails, some cells may grow out of proportion, and you get a tumor. If Mr. Greenspan keeps rising and lowering interest rates like a roller coaster to please various U.S. Presidents while disregarding basic economic rules, we (and the U.S. economy) will all get sick.

Next comes strategy. What is strategy? The word strategy derives from its Greek root, *stratos,* which means army, and the word egos, which, in this case, means leader. Strategy, in the original Greek, means "the art of the generals" or "the art of the leader of the army".

Strategos was a term used during a conflict, and it identified the ultimate ruler. This term did not apply to the captains or to the minor generals, but only to the top general who commanded the whole army—from recruiting to the army's supplies and support to its spies and to everything else that was going on during the military campaign.

The most important aspect of the new discipline of strategic planning is the ability, on the part of the executive (the man or woman on the top), to balance external analysis of relevant data with an inner sense of what constitutes the true purpose of the enterprise and the values it tries to fulfill in its environment. There needs to be a harmonious equilibrium between the need for the survival and growth of the organization and the need to satisfy the market's demand.

The lessons learned from the advocates of strategic planning can only emphasize the need for a holistic approach to planning. Leave something out of the main equation, and the results will not be satisfactory. Analysis should start from the most internal aspect of the organization—its purpose and corporate mission. Then, the strategist will move to study the environment in which the organization is operating, the analysis of the market being served, and the potential market intended by the organization's main goals and primary objectives.

Next, there must be an insightful study of all pertinent data in relation to the competition and to the competitive environment. A "military" strategic outlook, as that fostered by the Japanese industrial establishment, may have, at this point, some very positive advantages over a more naive outlook.

Finally, the last and most difficult job is that of "re-creating" and finding new, innovative ways to redefine the whole set of internal and external factors, so as to find a better way to: 1. Fulfill the mission of the enterprise, 2. Satisfy the needs of the consumer (client or market), 3. Improve the organization's position in the marketplace, and 4. Secure the prosperity and continuity of the organization at all levels (stockholders, management, employees and, where applicable, customers and suppliers).

The strategist remains a unique individual, at home both in the external world of analytical data, statistics, marketing, and management science, as well as in the inner world of corporate mission and vision: understanding human values, predicting future desires and needs, sensing priorities in operations, using intuition in marketing, expressing love and concern for the people within the organization (the corporate family), for the products or services rendered, for the people responsible for the organization's existence and success (the customer), and finally, for the environment in which the enterprise performs its activities.

NETWORKS

Not the telephone kind

Networks. It's one of the most widely used buzzwords in today's economy. Why? The idea of a network is as old as the world. The advent of the Internet and the expansion of the World Wide Web have created a real, functioning, global network.

Networks allow groups of people to work with a common focus, multiple and reinforced motivation, and a wealth of diverse skills, in order to achieve a shared goal.

To achieve success a network of people needs a basic structure with: 1. Unified purpose, goal, and vision, 2. Motivated members, 3. Effective links and communication, 4. At least one responsible leader, and, 5. A good plan.

The business that understands the best way to use a network has a distinct organizational advantage. The strategist, or a small group of founders, begins with a compelling vision. Next, the leader begins to look for talent. He or she starts to recruit people, hopefully the right people. Next come communication and the sharing of more specific goals, objectives, and tasks. With it comes the identification of the major actors (the people with the responsibility for the achievement of limited goals), the primary territory (market), and the rules, the values (priorities), and the time frame needed for completing the mission.

Military operations are among the best forms of networking effectiveness and efficiency (that's why Ross Perot, former head of EDS and long time Presidential hopeful, favors hiring people with some military experience). The military has also a powerful way to present its purpose. Today, many companies recognize the importance of vision and goals, and so they display their mission statements on TV commercials, on banners, on lapel pins, on buttons, and on other more or less explicit ways. (What's next? Tattoos?.)

Some Internet consultant said that purpose pulls people together. But missionary zeal is not enough. Regular drills, motivating goals, simple and clear rules and regulations, constant feedback, and, most important of all, the knowledge of being all part of the same unit (the same team or community) are some of the elements that make a military network all the more proficient (and they can do the same for you).

The CEO of a large Italian company (and leader of an Italian political party) for whom I did some consulting told me that, once his people learned to act and interact in a non-antagonistic way toward one another, the program they were working on took off like a rocket. If necessary, the leader of the network can act just as a facilitator, a teacher, or a consultant. The important thing is for the group to share the same vision, goals, values and norms. Cooperation is needed instead of competition. By the way, the word co-operation comes from operating together, while competition comes from "co-petitioning", that is begging for something standing next to another beggar. Which one do you prefer?

Did you ever dive near some rocky reef to look at that wonderful underwater world? In nature, successful networks (like those found in coral reefs) come into being because there are clear and tangible benefits in the sharing of tasks. People form networks around needs. When an individual or a group finds a way to meet a real need (Mr. Henry Ford's Model "T"), the larger community then finds a way to get its need satisfied, sharing their hard-earned dollars with the lucky innovators (in this case, the Ford Motor Company).

Needs and purpose provide the reasons for action. Sometimes, in the face of rapid change, traditional control mechanisms falter (or break down, like during the French Revolution of 1789). Communal needs may replace traditional authority and may even overpower brutal coercion and fear (like the collapse of the Berlin Wall).

Shared needs and a unifying goal are the most powerful energies at our disposal. Needs, goals and relations—just like values—may be difficult to locate. They may seem vague and intangible, but they are the glue that binds people together; their relationships are real, and they determine the behavior of the individuals and the group.

CONFLICT

How the wrong perceptions intensify conflict

If you are familiar with Stephen Covey's book, *The Seven Habits of Very Successful People*, you may remember the drawing of the young-and-old lady and the exercise that highlights the role of partisan perceptions. The task consists of looking at a line drawing that has in it two equally distinct, but vague, blurred pictures: that of an old woman, sad and looking down, and that of a young woman, looking away. Before showing the line drawing to a group of people, half the group is *predisposed* to see the old woman and half, to see the young woman. This was done by showing half of them a sharp drawing, emphasizing the old woman, while the other half of the group is shown an equally sharp drawing of the young woman. The results are that, almost always, one half of the group sees only the version of the picture they had been predisposed to see.

Often, without understanding the other's perceptions, individuals try to persuade each other that the woman in the picture is young or old, eighteen or eighty, beautiful or not, looking this way or that way. They almost always try to convince the others without success. Some people ask where the trick is.

When it is explained and they are shown the other possible way of looking at the drawing, some people are simply stunned.

This exercise was done among a group or Israeli officials. Someone said, "If I could be predisposed, in thirty seconds, to see an ambiguous picture only one way, just think what thirty years of relentless propaganda has done to us, both Israelis and Palestinians."

When the Israeli official, who had been trying to persuade his colleague that the woman was eighty and not eighteen, was asked whether it would have been different if he had been performing the exercise with a Palestinian, he said, "That would have been much easier. I would simply have dismissed without difficulty anything he said, assuming he was lying or trying to con me in some way."

The real ploy of this exercise is that there is no trick. Sometimes, even thirty seconds of seeing things one way can cause us to see things only that way. *A lifetime of perceiving things one way predisposes us to see only what we expect to see.*

The problem is that this predisposition is particularly true for those caught up in a conflict, where emotions run high (whether an Israeli or a Palestinian, an Irish Catholic or a Protestant, a black or a white American). Dealing with conflict means coping and understanding the way other people perceive, think, and feel.

On September 9, 2001, two days before the tragic events of 9-11, I met Shimon Peres at an economic convention (the Abrosetti Forum) in Cernobbio, Italy. During one of his speeches, Peres talked about human rights and stated, "The first and most fundamental right is life, without which none of the others have meaning."

But even if any reasonable person would share his logic, unfortunately, the way we humans perceive and value is quite often *not* ruled by logic. There is little doubt that, under harsh conditions, the value of freedom (or what some people consider such) can easily overpower the value of life itself.

From the dawn of human civilization, many freedom fighters,

including early Israeli patriots (from Gideon to Bengurion), chose to place freedom above the value of their own lives (and for sure above the lives of their enemies). So, the phenomena of the suicide bombers should not shock us so much. During the last wars (from Korea to Vietnam), the U.S. Army "asked" many U.S. soldiers to "volunteer" for missions with "very high risk." During World War II, many Jews would have gladly sacrificed their lives for even a small chance to kill Adolf Hitler. A general may sacrifice his best platoon to save a division.

So, what's new? *What is new is the targeting of defenseless civilians.* The cowardice shown by recent terrorists is foreign even to primitive tribes and primitive times, when the warriors of one clan did battle with the warriors of the enemy clan—not with defenseless women and children.

Some social commentators have said that for some, often more isolated cultures, the sole thought that they are losing their traditional control over the social body, and especially over the bodies of women, is intolerable. It is transformed into hatred of any outside influence which threatens that control. The degree of hatred is directly proportional to the desire for control over women, which explains why some other cultural groups, equally isolated, are not terrorists. The Taliban doubtless represented this fear to an extreme degree, whence their obsession with prohibiting access to all communications media while simultaneously loading up on the most sophisticated of modern armaments. Technology is bad if it could sap their control; it is good if it reinforces it.

Solutions often start from showing to the opposing party the other's views and perceptions and by reducing the level of irrational emotions involved. Most people think and feel differently from one another. The issue should not be whose perceptions are "right" and whose are "wrong" but rather if the parties involved can agree on a set of mutual needs (like the need *not* to slaughter each other). The opponents can then move from mutual needs on to mutual values (life, prosperity, peace), and then on to agreeable rules of conduct and behavior. Easy to say— a lot harder to do!

Thus, the better we understand the way people (including ourselves) perceive things, the better we will be able to deal with others. Of course, this takes a special effort in humility, but I hope that the tools and techniques suggested here can make the task of reducing conflict a little easier.

When we try to apply these findings to the task of governing a society, we find that the guiding policy should be clear and simple: the purpose of government (among others) is the prevention (through laws and enforcement agencies) of exploitation, harm, or injury among its people. This principle has been stated clearly and concisely in the words of Thomas Jefferson (already quoted before): *"The purpose of government is to prevent men from injuring one another."*

When applied as a guiding policy to a government, preventing harm to others may be viewed as one aspect of man's quest for Liberty, since its application should result in the maximization of the individual freedoms of its citizens. It is a rule as old as humanity (even if not always remembered). It reflects age-old ideals of mutual respect, justice, and fair dealings among members of the human race. It is the foundation of all major religions (from the Ten Commandments to the Eight-fold Path, from the Sermon on the Mount to the Holy Qumran), and it suggests that we should deal with others as we wish others to deal with us.

We are far from the end of history announced by Fukuyama. In fact, I believe we will never get there. Small nations will continue to exist, and so will large ones. Globalization will go hand in hand with movements stressing ethnic and regional identities. Someone has posed the hypothesis that terrorism will accelerate the processes of globalization, pushing Western nations (Fukuyama's liberal forces) beyond the phase of wild capitalism without faith or law, and into a phase of global political management as a condition of survival. The great powers find themselves forced to do what serious analysts have long known must urgently be done: regulate the sale of arms, control the laundering of money and other anti-government activities, regulate migratory flows, harmonize policies between countries, manage common resources and environment, etc. In brief, to put political and social order into the anarchy of an economy which has become detached from its humanitarian roots.

In conclusion, a good leader (in the fields of economics as well as politics) is an enlightened individual, not just a good strategist and a good entrepreneur, but one who knows the heart of the people and the unwritten rules that guide and inspire our innermost selves.

END NOTES

Corporate strategy

Strategic planning began its formal introduction to the corporate world in the early 1970s. Prior to this time, in the late '40s, '50s, and '60s, American management did not consider strategic planning as an essential tool to be used by the corporate executives. Often, planning went under the name of operations research or under the more general title of management.

Planning was thought of primarily as a function of product development, of area distribution, and as something that the research and development divisions would be more likely concerned with. Strategy, in the sense of data gathering and analysis, began to first find its way into the corridors of the U.S. intelligence community, where it had been brought during the Second World War (also with the help of the, then, more sophisticated British Intelligence). In the 1970s, with the worldwide oil crisis and the resultant shake-up of the corporate and financial world, businesses found it necessary to study possible plans of action and possible future scenarios, taking the example of some government agencies at the highest corporate level. For this reason, studies were initiated, and the area of strategic planning or corporate strategy came to the forefront of business schools all over the world.

Corporate strategy, as a modern idea, goes back to the writings of Peter Drucker, Kenneth Andrews and others. In 1965, Igor Ansoff said, "To use an engineering term, the strategic problem is concerned with establishing an impedance match between the firm and the environment or, in more usual terms, it is the problem of deciding what business the firm is in and what kind of businesses it will seek to enter."[15]

Also, in 1965, Professor Andrews wrote, "Strategy is the pattern of objectives, purposes, and goals, as well as major policies and plans for achieving these goals. These goals are stated in such a way as to define what business the company is in or is to be in and what kind of company it is or is to be."[16]

In the 1970s, the definition of strategic planning began to change. Economists started to focus more on the relationship between the firm and its environment. In 1978, Hofer and Schendel wrote, "The basic characteristics of the **match** an organization's purpose achieves with its environment is called its strategy."[17] In *The Structuring of Organizations* (1979), Mintzberg wrote, "Strategy formulation therefore involves the *interpretation of the environment* and the development of consistent patterns in streams of organizational decisions."[18] Similarly, M. Porter wrote in his *Competitive Strategy* (1980) that, "the essence of formulating competitive strategy is *relating* a company *to its environment.*"[19]

Little has changed in the following decade, and, in his 1988 edition of *Marketing Management*, Philip Kotler tells us that, "Strategic planning is the managerial process of developing and maintaining a viable fit between the organization's *objectives* and *resources* and its changing *market opportunities.* The aim of strategic planning is to shape and reshape the company's businesses and products, so that they combine to produce satisfactory profits and growth."[20] Recent literature has interpreted these early writings to indicate that one of the essential elements for corporate strategy is the relationship between the firm and its external environment.

Top managers, when thinking strategically and in a relational mode about their businesses, will automatically tend to identify themselves with the firm, as well as with the firm's environment.

The experienced manager and top executive will normally appraise and assess his actual and potential business organization based on the firm's inner strength, such as its assets—capital, product line, etc.,—as well as the firm's external environment, the so-called external opportunities in the Harvard School's SWOT system (strengths, weaknesses, opportunities, threats), as well as customers, suppliers, competitors, legal and political constraints, and so on. This approach, of defining Strengths and Weaknesses and Opportunities and Threats, has gained great popularity, thanks to the rush of Total Quality Management seminars and publications.

In conclusion, we could say that the task of the strategist is to find an ideal relationship or an ideal match between the firm (and its inner strengths) and its business environment (the external opportunities). This relationship must necessarily be consistent with the characteristics of that environment, as well as with the firm's own goals, objectives, resources, and capabilities.

The importance of purpose

Someone once said if you do not know where you are going, you won't go anywhere. So, why hurry if you can't figure out why you must run?

Just as values are determined by human desires and just as desires find their motivation in the goals and purposes of man, so it is in the area of strategic planning that vision, purpose, goals, and corporate mission do come first, ahead of organizational values and organizational behavior.

In the Value Theory: Purpose determines desires & needs. These, in turn, determine values & beliefs, which determine à behavior.

Similarly, *in Strategic Planning: Vision and Corporate Mission determine corporate goals, as well as organizational values; these, in turn, determine corporate behavior, projects, and activities.*

Strategically speaking, just like in the conceptual world of Plato's "Forms" and "Ideas," purpose and vision not only come first in terms of analysis, but they also come first in terms of importance. When preparing a strategic plan for the organization, the corporate executive needs to be very familiar with the corporate purpose and mission as well as with the spoken or unspoken vision of the organization's founders. Without such understanding of the overall vision and the specific purpose for which the organization exists, it is very difficult, if not impossible, to develop and implement an effective strategic plan.

Only after having analyzed vision, purpose, and mission, can the executive deal with the next set of categories, and this includes: 1. *Specific goals and objectives* (short and long-term), 2. The *time frame* involved in fulfilling those objectives, and 3. The *programs and activities* necessary to bring those projects to fruition.

The final stage, and an often-overlooked one in the strategic planning process, is that of evaluation and feedback. Without a constant and effective system of evaluation, and constant monitoring of both the programs and the objectives, it is not possible to decide if the strategic plan is working, or if it needs to be modified or improved. *Every living cell has a monitoring system through which data are constantly passed on to the nucleus for evaluation, and so every living creature receives constant feedback concerning its own subsystems (organs) and its environment.* It is here that Bill Gates, in his book, *Business @ the Speed of Thought*, hits the mark by equating an organization's information network to a nervous system.

It is interesting to notice how all practical applications of the concepts related to value theory, as well as corporate strategic plans (and even the direction of human development and progress), move from the conceptual world to the empirical world. Ideas and concepts (such as purpose, mission, vision) are first analyzed, dissected, and then put back together in a purely conceptual fashion. Only later will the strategist implement the conceptual elements of the plan in the material environment with concrete actions.

One important notion to be derived from the binary matrix

theory, as well as from practical observation, is that it is possible to divide purpose into two separate, but complementary, groups: the purpose for the one (the self), and the purpose relative to the community of which the one is a member (the many). Similarly, as we have done before, we can also divide any type of development into two complementary categories.

Conceptual (mental-emotional) —> Empirical (practical)
Internal (immaterial)   —> External (material)
Purpose & Goals   —> Programs & Activities
Thoughts & Emotions   —> Language & Behavior

And, like the proverbial two faces of a coin, both types of categories (internal and external, one and many) are interrelated, so that we can't have one without the other.

In the case of language, we should remember the importance of the spoken and written word. Language, emotions, thoughts and behavior are closely connected, and one can easily affect the others. Words can have a great power. Words can hurt or they can heal. In either case, words can have a deep impact on the psyche, the feelings and the behavior of human beings.

Returning to economics, while it is true that most companies' purposes is that of producing wealth and generating profits for their owners and stockholders, in the last two decades, small and large companies—such as Microsoft, IBM, EXXON, General Motors, and a host of others—have come to realize that the purpose of generating profit for the owners is not a sufficient motivation for the work and sales force, and it is not sufficient in generating a realistic corporate strategy and an effective, long-range marketing plan. For example, while some people may think that the purpose of IBM's existence is to generate profits for its owners and stockholders, top executives have long ago recognized that the main purpose for the existence of IBM is that of providing services and creating opportunities for the development of society. When Henry Ford, almost a century ago, started the manufacturing of the Model T Ford, his purpose was not necessarily only one of self-aggrandizement or personal wealth. Often, Henry Ford stated that his first desire was to provide a large segment of the population with the means of transportation that, at the time, were restricted to a very selected few, and *that thinking* is what made him successful.

We all know the joke that states that if Union Pacific Railroad would have understood that they were in the transportation business and not only in the railroad trade, today, we would be flying Union Pacific Airlines. Careful students and attentive researchers of corporate success in the United States have clearly seen the direct relationship between success and the desire to serve others (and that means to fulfill the market's needs, wants and genuine desires.) On the opposite side, we can clearly see today how the "Dot-Com" bubble began to fizzle and burst when the greed of many "me-too" entrepreneurs overpowered common sense, business sense, and genuine fair play.

Applications

The problem of decision-making is of central importance, not only to the business executive and the economist. It is also one of the most important subjects in the field of politics, ethics, education, and in everyday life.

In Business Administration, thanks to the innovative developments of the last two decades and the incredible computer revolution in the workplace, decision-making processes have grown from an art to a science. The new and exciting field of strategic studies (strategic planning, strategic management, Total Quality Management, etc.) has elevated the decision-making process to a degree of effectiveness and precision never experienced before.

New tools of systematic analysis and model theory can produce a host of real alternatives among which the experienced executive can choose the most effective course of action or implement the most efficient operational programs.

It is of the utmost importance, however, that the data and the "facts" collected and analyzed be arranged based on the right assumptions. Assumptions are a sort of intuitive knowledge; they involve the process of taking a statement as if it was true before it is proven to be so. In "assuming" (sorry for the repetition), we take chances. We risk that the strategy and the plan may or may not work, depending on the correctness of our assumptions. Assumptions must be very closely examined and judged critically before being used as the foundation for any hypothesis. It is for these reasons that, in this book, certain basic assumptions have been reviewed, and the need for a new set of assumptions has been established.

At all times and in every place around the world, organizations and institutions have developed cultures of their own, and success has often been closely tied to the ability to conform.

Often, the business culture of most corporations exalts logic, rationality, and conformity. Because of this, it is usually analysts rather than innovators who tend to climb the corporate ladder. This necessity to conform to the institutional culture has been one of the causes of stagnation and creative decline. Governments and societies (such as communist nations and countries where there is a high rate of ineffective bureaucracy) have also witnessed stagnation and decline.

Here in America, the pressure of innumerable social and governmental constraints on business activities has often put a premium on adaptation and has reduced even further, particularly with the proliferation of government regulations during the '60s and '70s, the incentive to innovate. Advocates of new, bold, and different strategies are too often relegated to the sidelines and labeled as troublemakers or eccentrics, while the system rewards those more skilled at complacency and conformity. These statements are particularly true in more mature industries (automobile, steel, petrochemicals, transportation, etc.) or government agencies, where actions and ideas often move slowly and within narrow aisles (if they move at all), keeping out innovations and sometimes progress itself.

Knowledge is not just data gathering. Ancient and medieval astronomers collected incredible amounts of precise information about the stars and the solar system, but, because of their incorrect assumptions (about the earth being flat, or at the center of the universe), their frame of reference was wrong, and, therefore, so were most of their conclusions.

The same thing happened to the top executives at IBM when, in 1977, a young Bill Gates signed a deal to *license* his new operating system. Similar things happened, and still do, to companies like Xerox, General Motors and others that were slow in recognizing changing paradigms.

Alvin Toffler, an American futurologist, wrote that the most important economic development of our lifetime has been the rise of a new system for creating wealth, based no longer on muscle but on mind, and that Knowledge, is the key to economic growth in the 21st century. The beacons of productivity and innovation, focused on the welfare of society, should be our guideposts. In looking at knowledge applied to human work as the source of wealth, we see a more correct function of the economic organization. Today, we have noticed a new approach, one that makes economics a more "human" discipline and relates it to human values, we see theories that give business leaders a yardstick to measure whether they are still moving in the right direction and whether their results are real or virtual. We are on the threshold of post economic theory.

But it is not enough to say that the essence of value is solely knowledge, as Drucker and Toffler said; the essence of value is the creative power of human beings. Knowledge is merely an element contributing to the creative power. What Marx called labor power is a "form" of creative power. There are two aspects of creative power: the mind, the idea, the emotional stimulating force, and the active, material, physical act. When both of them unite, focused on a single purpose, then we have maximum power and creativity. Marx's avoidance of use value and his assertion that only raw human labor formed value was fatally mistaken. Human labor manifests its creativity in dual fashion. Therefore, also the essence of a commodity reflects this binary creativity, and the value of commodities (a music CD, a car, a coffee cup, a book), and how much use value has been included in the commodity, are also manifested in the process of production. The value of a commodity is not determined solely by the quantity of labor, as Marx wrote more than 150 years ago. Marx's labor theory of value has meaning only when creativity (the inner aspect of labor) is minimal or absent. This occurs in crude production processes where labor is simple and its technology is unimportant. Today, the fallacies of Marxist theories have been amply demonstrated by the tragic collapse of the former Soviet Union. Regrettably, in many nations from Europe to Africa, hordes of former communist sympathizers still refuse to acknowledge the total failure of communist and socialist economic fantasy. Unfortunately, the greed of some corporate financial officers and CEO's (Enron), and the lack of concern for the community at large and the environment, continue to provide the pretext for the finger-pointing, blame and accusation of the so-called socially responsible left wings.

Future direction

In spite of continuous world economic growth and technological advances, more than half of the global population lives in a state of virtual poverty. Masses of people in East Asia, Africa, Latin America, and India live in conditions so limited by malnutrition, illiteracy, disease, polluted surroundings, infant mortality, and low life expectancy that are beneath any reasonable definition of human decency.

The once separate issues of environment and economic development are now inseparable. Poverty has become an agent of ecological degradation.

It is absolutely necessary to find a new, more enlightened vision of the future if we are to survive these challenges. We need to reformulate the basic economic questions with new and more holistic assumptions and norms. Such questions ask: 1. What other sources of energy are available in order to power society? 2. If it is not ecologically sound to continue to clear forests to grow limited food supplies, what other environment can produce the gigantic quantities of food necessary to sustain an exploding world population? (The oceans and intensive aquaculture seem a good bet.) 3. What should be done with the growing masses of poverty-stricken families? (Massive education, instead of famine relief, seems a better and more lasting initiative.)

There is little doubt that the ecological and population challenge will continue during the next decades. This is why it is necessary for economists and future forecasters to quickly develop an alternative to today's prehistoric assumptions and antiquated norms of economic theory. The key to a valid and effective economic system lies in the development and implementation of a globally acceptable system of economic values and accepted norms of economic behavior. Without a systematic framework for action, solutions to present and future problems will only be temporary and limited. It is only by taking into consideration the whole global system, both human society and its natural environment, that we might be able to discover lasting solutions to the mess we have created. Only by finding agreement on the most basic common values and norms (cultural and otherwise) can we lay the foundation for global cooperation and peace.

CHAPTER V

JOSEPH CAMPBELL

The power and value of legends and ideals

Joseph Campbell was probably one of the world's foremost authorities on mythology. Campbell taught Comparative Mythology for almost 40 years at Sarah Lawrence College, where a Chair in Comparative Mythology was established in his honor. His works, which include *The Hero with a Thousand Faces*, *The Masks of God*, and *Atlas of World Mythology*, have had a profound influence on millions of readers.

Campbell's work is immersed in questions of "value," primarily cultural and religious, but, as he stated in *The Power of Myth*, "We are so engaged in doing things to achieve purposes of outer (material) value that we forget that the inner value (cultural, spiritual, and philosophical) is associated with being alive." In other words, it is not possible to separate the study of material and economic values from their cultural and conceptual counterparts.

Campbell goes on: "The democratic ideal of the self determining individual, the development of the scientific method of research, the advent of the industrial age, and most recently the coming of the computer age has so transformed human life and society that most of the ancient symbols and the values associated with them have collapsed."

In his successful work, Joseph Campbell tries to point the way for modern man towards a more meaningful future. Campbell, particularly in his book, *The Hero with a Thousand Faces*, tries to indicate the desperate need of leading society to a new revival, that is, toward the creation of a new, global set of inner values. In all his works, Campbell tries to lift up the reader to meet the highest moral, ethical, and cosmic questions that have challenged mankind for ages. His answer is not one of a return to the golden age or even a rebirth or renaissance of ancient value systems.

What Campbell tried to discover, hidden in old myths and modern legends, were the values, symbols, and essential elements that are common to all men and women, in ancient times as well as today. Archetypes come from our common psyche, like dreams, and all men and women, in one form or another, have them. While ancient men tried to find answers through symbols and legends and myths, modern men have been forced to set aside all those beautiful metaphors and symbolic images and replace them with some sort of scientific explanations. Just like dreams, science is full of symbols, and science is also full of dreams and nightmares.

Naturally, science has not been able to answer all of man's existential questions. Our global society is still in a fluid state of transition. What we need today, and what Campbell tried to paint to his reader with colorful stories, is a set of global values—not only symbolic values, but also realistic, factual, and essential values around which man can build a better society.

Different cultural value systems and contrasting traditions are facing each other every moment in newspapers, magazines, and on television screens the world over. As the world becomes more like a single global village, thanks to the increased speed and ease of transportation and communication, we will continue to witness an unequivocal unification of values. The automatic result of this continuous exposure to different cultures is the alignment and leveling-off of global values and the development of a "common denominator" (a system of globally acceptable values and norms of behavior—a common value matrix).

SEVEN HABITS

Right, but not enough

Stephen R. Covey's long lasting bestseller, *The Seven Habits of Highly Effective People,* starts with an introduction on paradigms and principles. Covey tells us that, to change ourselves, we must first change our perceptions. I concur, but I would go one step further. Before we change our perceptions, we must have a better and more profound understanding of the way we perceive, and this Covey does not provide.

Another important step in Covey's book is the distinction between private and public victories. Covey identifies three principles dealing with the benefit to the individual, and three dealing with the benefit to the public. For private victory, be pro-active, begin with the end in mind, and put first things first. In the public victory field, think win-win, seek first to understand, then to be understood, and employ synergetic and creative cooperation. Finally, we find a final step of renewal, a view to evaluate results and "sharpen the saw."

Yes, Character Ethic may try to teach effective and righteous living, but it does not explain why we should follow the so-called foundations of success, such as Integrity, Industry, Temperance, and the Golden Rule. Yes, yes, we all know that it makes sense to practice rules that warrant the safety and development of the group. Can you imagine what would happen on a busy, undivided highway if we could not trust the cars coming on the opposite side to keep on their side of the road? But where do the Golden Rule and all other good moral rules come from?

Unlike Covey, I suggest that some of the so-called personality and character principles can be explained by the very inborn nature of human (and other living) beings. The great world religions are certainly full of wisdom in this respect, having always touched the deepest and often noblest aspect of the human heart and mind. What I'm trying to do is simply systematize the greater wisdom of giants gone before me in such a way as to understand better the deeper workings of the human mind and heart.

Balancing our concerns for ourselves (the one) and for the community (the many) is the *right* thing to do because that is in line with the way we perceive and categorize all things. Harmony comes from reconciliation with the very nature of our own being.

For Covey, *only basic goodness* gives life to success. His fault, if any, is that of relying too much on religious faith. Covey seems to forget that quite a few not-so-good sons of their mothers, like Hitler, Stalin, Genghis Khan, Attila the Hun, etc., were also very effective and successful in their way. Sharks may not be regarded as "good" or "moral", but they sure are effective and efficient.

Effectiveness is not the result of morality, just like science may or may not always agree with formal religious dogmas. Rather, I would suggest that we achieve greater and greater wisdom, and, therefore, effectiveness and success, as we reach deeper in the understanding of the nature of things—ourselves included.

As a teacher of strategic planning, Stephen Covey makes the connection between perception and value, but skips one step—that of categories. First, we need to study how the human being perceives.

From the study of how humans perceive, we have identified two sorts of categories. The first one is: me-world, one-many, inside-outside. From this first category, we derive a kind of symmetrical view of the world and what I call a relational framework. The second category is: binary relations. From the very first binary relation (me-world), human beings perceive the world as a multitude of relations, all of them reducible to their most simple binary form.

So, we clarify the distinction between inner and outer desires. After that, we make a distinction between our fundamental needs and desires for self-fulfillment and for individual happiness on one side, and, on the other side we look at the complementary, inborn, consideration for the well-being of our community. After looking at both sides of the proverbial coin, we then classify vision, purpose, and, finally, values. Only after organizing these topics can we see more clearly how values influence culture and behavior.

Finally, we can then work on *trying to modify some values in order to modify behavior,* keeping in mind that not even Tony Robbins, Stephen Covey, or the Pope can modify what is written in our DNA.

GENIUS

Where it comes from?

Some time ago, I read one of the most interesting articles, "Where does genius come from?" The article was published by the World Future Society in its monthly magazine, *The Futurist.* Unfortunately, I did not keep track of the issue or the authors, and for this I beg their pardon. Here are some of their findings:

Studying notebooks, correspondence, conversations, and ideas of some of the world's great thinkers, some scholars had identified a few types of thinking styles that seemed to empower talented individuals into generating a variety of innovative and original ideas. The authors of the article found some interesting similarities among individuals considered top in their field, from Leonardo Da Vinci to Albert Einstein and Thomas Edison.

First of all, they observed that *a genial idea often comes from finding a new perspective, that is, looking at something in a way no one else has before.*

Leonardo Da Vinci believed that, in order to gain knowledge about the form of a problem, one must begin by restructuring it in different ways. Da Vinci taught his students that the initial way we look at a challenge is often too biased towards the usual way we perceive things. He advocated reshuffling the puzzle and looking at it from one perspective and then moving to another point of view, and then to still another. With each new outlook, Da Vinci's (and our) understanding would deepen, and he would begin to understand the essence of the problem. He was able to see relationships between seemingly unrelated events and draw flying machines, helicopters, and parachutes hundreds of years before they were built.

Even Einstein's theory of relativity is, in a way, a description of the same phenomena viewed from different perspectives (sometimes light is perceived and acts as particles, other times as waves). Freud's interpretation of dreams (and his study of the subconscious mind) did not fit with the conventional view of his time. Looking at things from a different perspective may solve an existing problem, but it may also identify hidden ones.

When prehistoric men first tooled with agriculture, some innovative soul refused to answer the tribe's question on "how to get to the water." He asked, "Why can't we get the water to come to us?" So, be original, ask awkward questions, and try to raise questions that have not been asked before. (Be brave; *The Matrix* was just a movie!)

Skills in visual and spatial abilities provide the flexibility to display information in diverse and unique ways (if you cannot capture your web surfers' visual attention within two or three seconds, they'll click away to other sites). Leonardo Da Vinci's works are so accessible because he was able to put his thoughts into such beautiful pictures for the rest of the world to see. For him, the eye was truly the window of the soul, and, like a child, he visualized the most remote regions of his imagination. We are told also that Einstein, when he was wrestling with a problem, found it often necessary to use visual examples, such as drawings and diagrams. *Visual skills provide the bridge from the inner reality of thoughts and emotions to the outer reality of matter and form.*

To get creative outputs, we must feed our brain lots of innovative inputs. Psychologists have found that, in the early years of a child's development, the quantity and quality of intellectual and sensual stimulation is crucial to the development of the mind. Ironically, some businesses urge their employees to "think out of the box" while detaining them in dark, colorless, small, lifeless cubicles. (Steve Jobs did a great job in changing the old parameters of work environment and business attire and continues to do a great job in design innovation. He is another true Renaissance man.)

Relational thinking is also a sign of genius. The authors of the study noticed that one particular style of thought stands out in any creative individual, and that is the ability to make juxtapositions between dissimilar subjects. This capacity to connect the unconnected enables them to see things others do not. *Geniuses like to think in opposites.* Physicist and philosopher David Bohm believed geniuses were able to think different thoughts because they could tolerate ambivalence between opposites or two incompatible subjects.

Albert Rothenberg, a noted researcher on the creative process, identified in his 1990 book, *The Emerging Goddess: The Creative Process in Art, Science, and Other Fields,* this ability in a wide variety of geniuses, including Einstein, Mozart, Edison, Pasteur, Conrad, and Picasso. Also, Aristotle considered metaphors (another form of relational thinking—a parallel between a fact and a symbol) as a sign of genius, believing that the individual who has the capacity to perceive resemblances between two separate areas of existence and link them together is a gifted individual.

This ability to hold the tension of seemingly opposite ideas comes with the willingness to take chances, to embrace uncertainty, even ambiguity and paradox, and to "boldly go where no man has gone before." Curiosity, like necessity, can also be seen as the mother of invention. Curiosity brings us to untouched shores; it shows us the hidden mysteries of the universe; it teases us like a young lover, but it also rewards us with boundless treasures.

Carl Sagan, writer, scientist and host of the highly acclaimed television show, *Cosmos*, used to say that human beings are "specks of cosmic dust," made of the stuff that stars are made of, coming from the stars and longing to return, to master those stars.

As children of the stars, we often look in the infinite space, like in a warm summer night sky, and find peace and comfort. Great musicians have said that the music comes to life in the empty space between the notes. When asked how he made his beautiful *Pieta* (the statue of the Virgin Mary holding in her arms her crucified Son), Michelangelo, the great 15th century painter and sculptor, answered that the statue was already in that block of marble, he had only to remove all the stone that had enclosed it.

We are made of cells and atoms . . . and of the immense space between them. Music is made of notes . . . and of the silence between them.

Fortunately, we are told that creative strategies can be learned. Sociologist Harriet Zuckerman discovered that six of Enrico Fermi's students won the Nobel Prize, just as he had. Ernest Lawrence and Niels Bohr each had four winning students. J.J. Thomson and Ernest Rutherford trained 17 winners.

These Nobel laureates were not only creative in their own right but were also able to teach others how to think creatively. Zuckerman's subjects testified that their most influential masters taught them different thinking styles and strategies rather than what to think. Hopefully, recognizing and applying these creative strategies will help us be more creative in our work and in our personal life.

FUTURE DIRECTIONS

Conclusion

Gary Fleisher decided to take a swim in the big swimming pool of his new house, located in the growing residential quarters of Marsport Five. Looking up at the faint blue dome that rose fifty meters above the roof of his two-story house, Gary thought about his grandfather, George, and how much Mars had changed since they first arrived twenty years ago, in 2039.

Now, the transparent domes were multiplying like crystal mushrooms. The gigantic city domes, some as high as 500 meters and almost a mile wide, were used mainly as protection from the Martian winds and dust, from ultraviolet radiation, and as a way to recapture oxygen leaks from the smaller domes. Inside the big domes there were smaller ones, covering buildings, private and government installations, and even individual homes like Gary's. Each smaller dome was self sufficient in terms of water and air.

The swimming pools were ideal holding tanks. The water was recycled and purified and used for growing food and oxygen-producing plants and algae. Machines underground did most of the mining and manufacturing.

The first explorers found some form of Martian microbes, but the UV reflective chambers, a kind of ultraviolet reflecting-light furnace (originally developed by Molecu-Care of Connecticut, in 2001), eliminated 99.9% of all pathogens, including hard-to-kill bacterial spores (something that came really handy in the bio-terrorist wars of 2020).

Through commerce and travel, the Moon and Mars colonies prospered, and Gary found himself marveling at how accurate his grandpa's predictions had been in that distant 2002.

Fantasy? Maybe. But even the most innovative science fiction writer of fifty years ago wouldn't have predicted the marvels that every day confront us, from genetics to integrated circuits and from medicine (did you read about the German team that repaired a damaged heart with stem cells) to software.

We still have a lot to do, particularly in transportation and distribution, but the nervous system of the global village is waking up, and, like a baby, the next to grow and mature will be its mobility, its coordination, and its intellectual abilities (past the so-called information age, we are now entering the *Age of Wisdom*).

This book does not pretend to give any final answer; it isn't a theory of everything. I just hope it has helped you understand the way we perceive and value, providing a framework upon which we can build a better economy and a better society.

I began this work trying to learn what makes people behave, looking for ways in which I could add "value" to my consulting job. I began by studying the way we perceive—the way we engage our senses and our thoughts. In doing so, I came across a simple way to organize thoughts and sensations: the binary matrix.

Using the binary matrix, I took you on a journey (hopefully, not too boring) through the concept of value, its motivating powers (needs and desires), and some of its applications in business (strategy) and in culture (behavior). If you found something good, great! Send me a note at my web address or recommend this book to your friends. If you didn't, try reading it again; maybe, you missed something. ·

Money is not the only possible measure of value and, to try to reduce every thing and every human activity to monetary (and thus numeric) values, limits greatly the economic horizon and distorts reality to a point that goes below the most basic function of human nature.

Mankind has proven, throughout the ages, that it doesn't know the limits to its creativity. And, while some economists try to convince us of our shortcomings and of our limitations, it would be helpful to remember that *human talent, creativity, adaptability, and courage (risk-taking) in the face of adversities have (eventually) always won over limitations, restrictions, ignorance, oppression, and fear.*

Self-centered and individualistic approaches breed conflict and stagnation; holistic and community-serving approaches to economic activity bring about synergetic energies. There is a natural tendency in human beings to share their abilities with others, and this brings about the best in people. Largent and Breton say it best: "Cross-pollinating our creative abilities makes economic exchange synergetic. Through exchange, diversity increases diversity. Knowledge, skill, and creativity feed each other to yield possibilities greater than what individuals alone could produce."[21]

After the events of September Eleven, there is a real danger that, without a new vision or a new set of globally acceptable values, American leadership may fall further into a sense of failure and insecurity, creating the conditions for hostile and unpredictable policies. The most essential item on the agenda of political and business leaders the world over, should be the immediate revival and renewal of ethical and moral principles and values.

What we need is no longer a value system set on parochial values, but one that reflects the true aspirations of different cultures and peoples. No longer do we need a value system centered solely on monetary values and materialistic principles, but a universal system centered on true human desires for both material and non-material needs.

It is no longer valid—the assumption that values be designed to serve the individual first and the community last; there cannot be a self-centered concern for one's own success and salvation ahead of the salvation of the whole community; rather, we need values that are shared by and protect both the community as well as the individual.

In a scene from the movie, *A Beautiful Mind*, the main character, John Forbes Nash, portrayed by Russell Crowe, has a flash of insight when he tries to explain to his fellow classmates how Adam's Smith's statement that "greater value is found when individuals find ways to serve the community's needs before one's own," could be improved by the rule that states that "an even greater value is found when individuals find activities that can serve both the individual as well as the community."

This is also a key corollary of the value matrix. Maximum value is obtained by combining what is good for the community to what is good for the individual.

Further subdivisions of economics and business management science into increasingly smaller disciplines will not make it easier for economists and business executives to make proper and sound decisions. It is more likely (and auspicial) that, in the future, a renewal of synergetic and synthetic approaches to both economics and managerial sciences and to economics and social sciences (particularly, behavioral theories and axiology) will be necessary for success.

Today, we witness a trend toward unifying these different disciplines in a general theory of economic and social science. Physicists are looking for a General Theory, one that can explain the relationship between different physical forces (such as the atomic force, the strong force, the electromagnetic force, and the gravitational force). Cosmologists are looking at distant galaxies and finding that interstellar and cosmic dusts are making the heavens more and more like a gigantic weather system. So, in the world of business, we need to find the unifying factors, the common values, and the basic principles that govern economics and management science.

The study of the basic principles of economics and the underlying philosophical, moral, and ethical values associated with the present economic system of free enterprise have been recently under close scrutiny and criticism. Not only the neo-classical price theory, but also contemporary capital and distribution theories, have been under attack. Other value theories, in the broadest sense of the word, have lost their appeal in our fast-changing, global village.

Economic value theory has been in a state of constant confusion from its classical, cost-of-production beginning. The Marxist moral challenge has not been clearly overcome, and, even though Communism is quickly becoming a forgotten word, capitalist societies have not yet found a morally valid and acceptable counterproposal to Marx's condemnation of the selfish nature of the capitalist system.

Criticism has been leveled against all: classical, Marxist, Neo-classical, and contemporary value theories. Often, the superficiality of their definition of value and the association of "value" with "price" have clearly neglected the more axiomatic elements associated with the determination of value, among which are human desires (love, passion, and market demand), and the purposes associated with them.

Economy and sociology are sciences essentially based on the concept of value. But, up to now, value has been primarily interpreted as the material "worth" of goods that are able to fulfill the physiological needs of society.

As society evolves, particularly in the last one hundred years, essential needs, such as food, shelter, and clothing, have been more easily satisfied (at least for large segments of the population of industrialized countries). Life may actually have become more interesting and challenging precisely because today we can tackle the question of purpose and shape our destinies more in accordance with our wishes.

Today we see the rise of new needs and new desires. Many of the wants of modern humans (such as intellectual achievement, entertainment, music, emotional and spiritual fulfillment, art, science, and education) are most often not of a material nature.

One and many are inexorably linked together, but, if in conflict, the good of the many must come before the good of the few, or of one. The benefit to the whole community, or the harm to it, must have priority over the profits to the few (Enron executives included). If we can, we should try for a win-win approach; otherwise, we must be clear about what is primary and what is secondary. Only by accepting and applying this basic principle may we be able to develop effective and efficient strategies and a functioning global economy.

What you can do

It was late at night in Marsport Five. Gary was sitting by the pool, staring at the night sky. "Without the hydrogen drive," thought Gary, "there would be no fast travel to Mars." There was a little known change in policy during the first Bush Jr. administration in January 2002, when the U.S. Government dropped a multi-billion dollar, high-mileage, gasoline-fueled project in favor of a plan to develop hydrogen-based fuel cells.

That laid the groundwork for the now omnipresent hydrogen motors, and the powerful interplanetary hydrogen drives.

Even seemingly small changes, when directed toward the benefit of the greater community, can have gigantic effects.

In this book, I have proposed the Binary Matrix as the model for categorizing value. But, the Matrix can be applied to a multitude of other categories.

Friedrich Hegel (1770-1831), one of the most influential thinkers of the 19th century, formulated a philosophy based on two antithetical elements: Thesis and Antithesis. Marx built on it by transporting Hegel's dualism to economics and to social behavior, suggesting the now infamous "struggle of the proletariat."

But tension (and union) between two complementary elements is nothing new. Buddhist teachings have been around long before Marx and Hegel, and they have described a world made of complementary, bi-polar elements.

The Binary Matrix does not pretend to be a new philosophy; it is just a new (and I believe more valid) interpretation of the way we, as human beings, perceive ourselves and the world.

It is essential to business because it shows the way we can understand where "value-added" comes from, how to produce value, how to add value to products and services, how to add value to our activities, and even (sorry, I got carried away) add value to our lives (by serving others, our communities and our progeny).

The two categories of Self and Others (One and Many) are seen only as the initial step that we use to categorize our perceptions and our experiences. From this basic binary construct, we associate the other two essential categories of inner and outer (the inner Self and the outer world). This is the nitty-gritty of the way we perceive, we value, and we judge people and things.

The Binary Matrix is just a tool—one that, I believe, is more adept and familiar to today's digital world. I am not proposing a new philosophy, I am just pointing out to a new (and old), easier, and more widespread (common to most humans) way to understand what's important (what's valuable) and why (where our needs and desires come from).

Eventually, a new system of thought (possibly one using a binary matrix) will arise to take up the challenge of the global civilization. We need a comprehensive ideology able to revitalize and redefine traditional values and principles. We need a catalyst that can harmonize capitalist economies and values (such as private and public property) with the growing communal needs of our multicultural, multi-valued world. A new system of common values will be able to bring, to both eastern and western societies, a new and common vision of the future: a globally acceptable concept of the values of truth, liberty, honor, justice, and a revived view of ethics.

I want to take the opportunity to congratulate the reader who has decided to stick with me until the end. I may not be able to meet you in person, but I like to thank every reader for having taken the time to go with me in this little odyssey through value theory. Most important, if these pages have been able to inspire or motivate even one person, my work will have been greatly rewarded (and, if they did inspire you and if it worked for you, do a good deed and tell a friend).

NOTES

END NOTES

[1] Some of Hobbes' famous expressions, such as *homo homini lupus* (every man is a wolf to another man) and *bellum omnium contra omnes* (life is like a war of all against all), have been turned into maxims describing the ruthless confrontation of mankind with the egotism of each separate individual.

[2] Smith, *Wealth of Nations.*

[3] Smith, *Wealth of Nations.*

[4] Smith, *Wealth of Nations.*

[5] Smith, *Wealth of Nations.*

[6] Tredennick, Hugh, *Plato: The Last Days of Socrates* (London: Penguin Books, 1954)

[7] Kennedy, Paul, *The Rise and Fall of the Great Powers* (New York: Random House, 1987)

[8] Smith, *The Wealth of Nations.*

[9] Smith, *The Wealth of Nations.*

[10] Largent and Breton, *The Soul of Economies.*

[11] Toyenbee, Arnold, *The Rise and Fall of Civilizations.*

[12] Largent and Breton, *The Soul of Economies.*

[13] Boulding, Kenneth, *Human Values and Economic Policy.*

[14] Particularly by A. Marshall and utilitarian marginalists.

[15] Igor H. Ansoff, *Corporate Strategy*, New York: McGraw Hill,

1965.

16 C. R. Christensen, K. R. Andrews, J. L. Bower, *Business Policy: Tests and Cases*, (Housewood, Ill.: Richard Irwin Publ., 1973).

17 C. W. Hofer, D. Schendel, *Strategy for Formulation: Analytical Concepts*, (St. Paul: West Publishing, 1978).

18 H. Mintzberg, *The Structuring of Organizations*, (Englewood Cliff, N.Y.: Prentice Hall, 1979).

19 M. Porter, *Competitive Strategy*, (New York: Free Press, 1980).

20 P. Kotler, *Marketing Management*, (Englewood Cliff, N. J.: Prentice Hall, 1988).

21 Largent and Briton, *The Soul of Economies.*

BIBLIOGRAPHY

Amey, Lloyd R., *Corporate Planning*. New York: Praeger Co., 1986.

Anderson, T. L. & Hill, P. J., *The Birth of a Transfer Society*. Stanford, CA.: Hoover Institution Press, 1980.

Ansoff, H. I., *Corporate Strategy*. New York: McGraw Hill, 1965.

Bell, Wendel, *Foundations of Future Studies*. New Brunwick, N.J.: Transacton Publishers, 1997.

Berlusconi, Silvio, *Il Libro Nero del Comunismo*. Milan: Mondadori Editore, 1998.

Bhagvan, Sri Sathya, *Upanishd Vahini*. Lakemont, Ga.: CSA Printing, 1970.

Becker, G. S., *The Economic Approach to Human Behavior*. Chicago: University of Chicago Press, 1976.

Bentham, Jeremy, *An Introduction to the Principles of Morals and Legislation*. New York: Hafner Publishing, 1948.

Breton & Largent, *The Soul of Economies*. Wilmington, Del.: Idea Publishing House, 1991.

Blackburn, John D., *The Legal Environment of Business*. Homewood, Ill.: Irwin Press, 1982.

Boehm-Bawerk, Eugen Von, *The Positive Theory of Capital*. New York: G.E. Stechert and Co., (1889) 1959.

Bodin, Jean, Supplements to *History of Economic Thought*. Cambridge, Mass.: Harvard University Press, 1924.

Bryson, John, *Strategic Planning*. San Francisco: Jossey Bass Publishing, 1989.

Boulding, Kenneth Ewart. *Beyond Economics: essays on society, religion and ethics*. Ann Arbor, University of Michigan Press, 1968.

Buckley, P., & Casson, M., *The Future of the Multinational Enterprise*. London: Croom Helm Ltd., 1981.

Bulgarelli, O., *Il Denaro alle Origini delle Origini*. Milan: Spirali Editori, 2001.

Carrison, Dan & Walsh, R., *Semper Fi. Business Leadership and the Marine Corp Way*. New York: AMACOM, 1998.

Campbell, Joseph, *The Power of Mith*. New York: Doubleday, 1988.

Chamberlain, Neil W., *Beyond Malthus*. New York: Basic Books Publishing, 1970.

Channon, D. & Jalland, M., *Multinational Strategic Planning*. London: McMillan, 1974.

Churchman, C. W., *The System Approach*. New York: Dell Publishing, 1968.

Cicerone, Marco Tullio, (Cicero), *Il Fato.(On Fate)*, original version and translation by Francesca Antonini, Rome. Italy: Rizzoli Editore, 1994.

Cobb, John B. & Daly, Herman, *For the Common Good: Redirecting the Economy Toward Community, the Environment and a Sustainable Future*. New York: Beacon Press, 1989.

Cook, Thomas M. & Russell, R., *Management Science*. Englewood Cliffs, New Jersey: Prentice Hall, 1985.

Covey, Stephen R. *The Seven Habits of Highly Effective People*. New York: Simon and Shuster, 1989.

Dalai Lama, *A Simple Path*. Thorson Publishers, 2000.

Darwin, Charles. *On the Origin of the Species, Norwalk, Ct.:* The Easton Press, 1963.

Davidson, W. H., *Global Strategic Management*. New York: John Wiley & Sons, 1982.

Denzin, N. K., *The Research Act*. New York: McGraw-Hill, 1978.

De Tocqueville, Alexis. *On Democracy, Revolution, and Society.* Chicago: University of Chicago Press, 1980.

Dewey, John, *Theory of Valuation.* Chicago: University of Chicago Press, (1939) 1972.

Dobb, M., *Theories of Value and Distribution Since Adam Smith.* Cambridge, Mass.: Cambridge University Press, 1973.

Donald, David H., *Lincoln.* Norwalk, Ct.: The Easton Press, 1996.

Druker, Peter F., *Management: Tasks, Responsibility, and Practices.* New York: Harper & Row, 1974.

Eichner, Alfred, *A Guide to Post-Keynesian Economics.* White Plains, New York: M. E. Sharpe, Inc., 1979.

Etzioni, Amitai, *The Moral Dimension: Toward a New Economics.* London: Macmillan, 1988.

Friedman, Milton, *Capitalism and Freedom.* Chicago: University of Chicago Press, 1962.

Friedman, Milton, *A Theory of the Consumption Function.* Princeton, New Jersey: Princeton University Press, 1957.

Friedman, Milton & Rose, *Free to Choose.* New York: Harcourt Press, 1980.

Fukuyama, Francis, "Are we at the end of history?" Fortune. January 15, 1990.

Gates, Bill. *Business @ the Speed of Thought.* New York: Warner Books, 1999.

Gingrich, Newt, *To Renew America.* New York: Harper Collins Publishers, 1995.

Gray, Alexander, *The Development of Economic Doctrine.* London: Longman's and Green Co., 1948.

Groff, Gene, *Operations Management.* Homewood, Ill.: R. Irwin, 1969.

Hafer, C. & Schendel, D., *Strategy Formulation: Analytical Concepts.* St. Paul: West Publishing Co., 1978.

Hagenaars, A. J., *The Perception of Poverty.* Amsterdam: North Holland Publishing Co., 1986.

Harman, Willis, *Global Mind Change: The Promise of the Last Years of the 20th Century.* Knowledge Systems, 1988.

Heilbroner, R. L., "Modern Economics in the History of Thought" Social Research Journal. Vol. 50, Summer, 1983.

Hicks, J. R., *Value and Capital*. 2nd Edition, Oxford, 1946.

Hollander, Samuel, *The Economics of Adam Smith*. Toronto: University of Toronto Press, 1973.

Huber, George, *Managerial Decision Making*. Glenview, Ill.: Scott, Forseman Co., 1980.

Hutchison, T.W., "The Bicentenary of Adam Smith," *Economic Journal*. September 1976.

Kash,Rick, *The New Law of Demand and Supply*. New York: Doubleday, 2002.

Kennedy, Paul, *The Rise and Fall of the Great Powers, Economic Change and Military Conflict from 1500-2000*, New York: Random House, 1987.

Keynes, J., *Essays and Sketches in Biography*, New York: Meridian Press, 1956.

Keynes, John M., *The General Theory of Employment, Interest, and Money*. New York: Harcourt, 1935.

Kotler, P., *Marketing Management*. Englewood Cliffs, New Jersey: Prentice Hall, 1988.

Kuhns, E. & S.U. Martorana, *Qualitative Methods for Institutional Research*. San Francisco, CA.: Jossey-Bass Publishers, 1982.

Landreth and Colander, *History of Economic Thought*. Boston: Boughton Mifflin Co., 1989.

Landes, David, *The Wealth and Poverty of Nations*. New York: W.W.Norton Company, 1998.

Layard, P. R. & Walters, A. A., *Microeconomic Theory*. New York: McGraw-Hill, 1978.

Leontiades J., *Multinational Corporate Strategy*. Lexington, Mass.: Lexington Books, 1985.

Lombardi, Guido G., *Liberta' e Benessere Economico*. Milan: Franco Angeli, 1998.

Luttwak, Edward. *Turbo Capitalism*. New York: Harper Collins, 1999.

Malthus, Thomas R., *An Essay on the Principle of Population.* Seventh Edition, 1872, New York: Augustus Kelley Publishing, 1971.

Marshall, Alfred, *Principles of Economics.* 8th Edition, London: McMillan Press, (1890) 1920.

Marx, Karl, *Capital.* 3 Vols. Translated by Samuel Moore and Edward Aveling. Moscow: Progress Publishers, 1956-1959.

Marx, Karl, *Contribution to the Critique of Hegel's Philosophy of Law.* MECW, Vol. 3.

Menger, Carl, *Principles of Economics.* New York : University Press, (1871) 1976.

Mermelstein, David, edited by, *Economics: Mainstream Readings and Radical Critiques.* New York: Random House, 1973.

Metzger, Michael B., *Business Law & the Regulatory Environment.* Homewood, Ill.: Irwin, 1986.

Mill, J. S., *Principles of Political Economy with some of their Applications to Social Philosophy.* New York: A.Kelley Press, (1848) 1976.

Mill, J. S., *On Liberty.* Norwalk, Connecticut: The Easton Press, 1991.

Mill, J. S., *Essays on Some Unsettled Questions of Political Economy,* Second Edition,. New York: A. M. Kelley, 1968.

Mill, J.S., *Collected Works of John Stuart Mill.* Toronto: University of Toronto Press, 1965.

Mintzberg, H., *The Structuring of Organizations.* Englewood Cliffs, New Jersey: Prentice-Hall, 1979.

Ohmae, K., *The Mind of the Strategist.* New York: McGraw Hill, 1982.

Paret, Peter, *Makers of Modern Strategy from Macchiavelli to the Nuclear Age.* Princeton, N.J.: Princeton University Press, 1986.

Patton, M.G., *Qualitative Evaluation Methods.* Beverly Hills, CA.: Sage Publishing, 1980.

Peters, T. & Waterman, B., *In Search of Excellence.* New York: Harper & Row, 1982.

Peters, Tom, *A Passion for Excellence.* New York: Harper & Row,

1982.

Peterson, William, *Malthus.* Cambridge, Mass.: Harvard University Press, 1979.

Peterson, M. D., *Thomas Jefferson and the New Nation.* Norwalk, Conn.: Easton Press.1970.

Porter, M., *Competitive Strategy.* New York: Free Press, 1980.

Ricardo, D., *On the Principles of Political Economy and Taxation.* Cambridge: Cambridge University Press,(1871) 1951.

Ricardo, D., *On the Principle of Political Economy and Taxation,* in *The Works and Correspondence of David Ricardo,* edited by P. Sraffa and M. Dobbs. Cambridge: Cambridge University Press, 1953.

Ricardo, D., *Notes on Malthus' Principle on Political Economy.* Cambridge: Cambridge University Press, 1957.

Samuelson, P. A., *Foundations of Economic Analysis.* Cambridge, Mass.: Harvard University Press, 1947.

Schumpeter, J. H., *History of Economic Analysis.* New York: Oxford University Press, 1954.

Senior, N. W., *An Outline of the Science of Political Economy,* New York: A. Kelley Publishers, 1951.

Shuster, George, *Saint Thomas Aquinas.* Norwalk, Conn.: Easton Press, 1995.

Sloan, A. P., *My Years with General Motors.* London: Pan Books, 1967.

Smith, Adam, *An Inquiry on the Cause of the Wealth of Nations* (1776). New York: The Modern Library, 1994 Edition.

Smith, Adam, *The Theory of Moral Sentiments.* (1759) Reprint, New Rochelle, New York: Arlington House, 1969.

Smith, Adam, *Adam Smith's Moral and Political Philosophy.* New York: Harper and Row, 1970.

Smith, W.H., *Strategies of Social Research: The Methodological Imagination.* Englewood Cliffs, N.J.: Prentice-Hall, 1975.

Spence, Gerry. *Give Me Liberty.* New York: St Martin's Griffin, 1998.

Stigler, G., "The Development of Utility Theory," *Journal of Political Economy,* 1950.

Stigler, George, "Ricardo and the Ninety Three Percent Labor Theory of Value," *American Economic Review*, 1958.

Steiner, A. & Miner, J. B., *Management Policy and Strategy*. New York: McMillan, 1977.

Sun Tsu, *The Art of War*. Translated by Samuel Griffith. Norwalk, Ct.: The Easton Press, 1988.

Taylor, R. & Rosenbach, W., *Military Leadership*. Boulder, Co.: Westview Press, 2000.

Titus, H.H. & Smith, Marilyn, *Living Issues in Philosophy*. New York: Van Nostrand Co., 1974.

Tredennick, H., *Plato: The Last Days of Socrates*. London: Penguin Books, 1954.

Von Mises, Ludwig, *Economic Policy*. Washington, D.C.: Regnery Gateway, 1979.

Von Mises, Ludwig, *Human Action: A Treatise on Economics*. Chicago: Contemporary Books, 1949.

Varian, H., *Microeconomics Analysis*. New York: Norton Publishers, 1978.

Waddington, C. H., *Operations Research in World War II, or Against the U-Boat*. London: Paul Elek Publishing, 1973.

Walras, L., *Elements of Pure Economics or the Theory of Social Wealth*. Elmwood, Illinois: Richard Erwin Press, 1954.

Yeltsin, Boris, *Against the Grain*. New York: Summit Books, 1990.

7889885R0

Made in the USA
Charleston, SC
19 April 2011